Peanut Butter Kisses & Mud Pie Hugs

Becky Freeman

HARVEST HOUSE PUBLISHERS
Eugene, Oregon 97402

Cover by Koechel Peterson & Associates, Minneapolis, Minnesota

PEANUT BUTTER KISSES AND MUD PIE HUGS
Copyright © 2000 by Becky Freeman
Published by Harvest House Publishers
Eugene, Oregon 97402

Library of Congress Cataloging-in-Publication Data
  Freeman, Becky, 1959–
    Peanut butter kisses and mud pie hugs / Becky Freeman
      p. cm.
    ISBN 0-7369-0240-6
    1. Motherhood. 2. Motherhood—humor. I. Title.
HQ759.F743   2000
306.874'3—dc21   99-085707
                                                                              CIP

  00 01 02 03 04 05 06 07 08 09 / BP / 10 9 8 7 6 5 4 3 2 1

Remembering Erma

I talk to women a LOT. And they talk to me. A LOT. This one thing I know for sure, gleaned from hundreds of conversations: I'm not alone in missing Erma Bombeck. There was some sort of universal comfort in knowing she was somewhere tripping up and making messes on this planet, right along with us. In some small way, I feel I'm honoring her memory every time I blow it and find a way to view it as funny. Her columns and books were Motherhood Survival Tools for me right along with prayer and friends and a well-worn Bible. (The same, I know, is true for my own mother and grandmother. Her column clippings—what we called "Erma's Latest Funnies"—were mailed back and forth between the females in my family, tucked inside handwritten letters, for years.)

I once wrote Erma a letter while she was going through the painful process of kidney dialysis, and she graciously wrote back saying, "Dear Becky, I cannot begin to tell you how much your kind letter meant to me. I am doing well and am ready to start writing yet another book. As George Burns once said, 'I can't die. I'm booked.'" Somehow I believed her, but then, I guess we all know, deep inside, that God is not tied to our plans, however well-laid they may be.

Erma also hand-scribbled a note saying that she'd love to see my new book (my first manuscript had just been accepted). Sadly, she didn't live long enough for me to share that joy with her.

The day Erma died, I received four or five phone calls from friends beginning, "Becky, I just knew you'd be hurting…" or "I know how much you loved Erma's writing…"

Erma was Every Neighbor, Every Mom, Every Best Friend to a nation of women who needed to laugh as badly as their bathrooms needed scrubbing. As badly as they needed to lose 20 pounds. Most of us still have pounds to lose, and a ring around the tub…but, thanks to Erma, we're laughing anyway.

We loved her from afar. We miss her every time we open a Sunday paper. To her husband and children, thank you for letting us "borrow" Erma now and again as she burnt the pot roast while finishing up a great line or a funny story. Nothing will erase the pain of your great loss. But I hope that the passage of time, God's loving presence, and knowing that her work is still inspiring other moms to laugh (and some, like me, to write) will be a comfort. No one can write family humor like Erma. I doubt anyone ever will. She was in a class all her own.

But if this book can make one tired mother, at the end of her parenting rope, crack a smile, it's my prayer that God and Erma will join in with laughter from heaven.

In Erma's last column, written the day after my thirty-seventh birthday, April 17, 1996, she wrote:

My deeds will be measured not by my
youthful appearance,
but by the concern lines on my forehead,
the laugh lines from around my mouth,
and the chins from seeing what can be done for those
smaller than me who have fallen.

May this be so for all of us mothers. Indeed, Lord, may it be so.

Acknowledgments

First and foremost, I must thank my amazing, hilarious, sweet, and talented sister, Rachel, for serving as my assistant editor—and diving in with huge doses of help on this project.

Secondly, I want to praise my family for being fabulous sports about having a "creative wife and mother" and graciously letting her watch you like a vulture, scoping for material.

Thirdly, I want to thank my wonderful agent and beloved brother in Christ, Greg Johnson, for great advice, an encouraging spirit, and a tender heart. And for always reminding me to keep my Lord and my family first, even if it means turning down good opportunities.

Thank you to Chip MacGregor for making me laugh so hard that I sometimes snort in a decidedly UNfeminine manner—and for going to bat for this project with the nice folks at Harvest House. Special gratitude to Betty Fletcher, a first-rate editor, as well as to Harvest House First Ladies, Carolyn McCready and LaRae Weikert. (I don't yet know what they officially "do" but they sure are a lot of fun.)

To Brenda Waggoner, Gracie Malone, Melissa Gantt—for being the ever-ready "village" of ladies brave enough to be my friends, lunch pals, and e-mail editors.

To Rose, my personal assistant, who cheerfully reminds me what I'm doing when I forget. (Which is often.)

To Gene and Carol Kent, my speaking agents, mentors, cheerleaders, and praying friends.

To the memory of Bob Briner, consummate "Roaring Lamb"—whose life, well lived, and words, well spoken, sprinkled this woman's heart with the salt of Christ's love.

And of course, thank you to my father for his unswerving love and belief in me, and to my own mother, Ruthie Arnold, for the warm peanut butter cookies, cool washcloths, and late-night prayers through the years. Oh yes—and for teaching this daughter how to laugh at herself and write about it to boot!

Contents

Part I
A Child Is Born
(& Will It Be the Death of Me?)

Part II
Days of Whine & Noses

Part III
Home for Bewildered Mothers

Part IV
Teenagehood
(or "The Toddler Reprise")

Part I

A Child Is Born

(& Will It Be the Death of Me?)

1

Irrational Conception

I often wondered why our best "couple" friends, Dean and Heather, continued to invite us over. Their peaceful home was uninhabited by small children, and their lifestyle was one of freedom and serenity. For six years, I waddled into their immaculate home, eternally pregnant and holding at least one toddler and/or a rambunctious child by the hand. It seemed that every time I thought my child-bearing years were over, the dot would turn blue—and I would, too. At least temporarily. After observing the reality of parenthood, up close and personal, Dean and Heather had definitely decided not to have children, and that was semifinal.

Yet Heather seemed genuinely intrigued with us. She always plied me with questions, like a reporter gathering information from some lost Aboriginal tribe. She seemed to find it absolutely fascinating that I could survive four small children amid a life of total disarray and still smile occasionally—even *frequently*.

They were the perfect yuppie host and hostess, cooking side by side and serving scrumptious meals together. But once our brood dropped off to sleep, Scott and I reveled in the soft background music drifting from the stereo and the uninterrupted and oh-so-adult conversation. Strangely, it often drifted to the Big Question: "What's a good reason and when is a good time, if ever, to have a baby?"

I struggled to find a way to answer their question because, as the old quote goes, "To decide to have a child is to choose to have your heart go walking around outside your body forever." And yet, it somehow increases the size of your heart. Children give depth to our lives. Like those magic pictures that seem one-dimensional, until you move in closer, cross your eyes, and discover there's more there than you'd ever imagined. Children give shape, color, and texture to everything we do and see. Christmas morning comes alive with sheer joy as a child's rubber-soled, pajamy feet come shuffling expectantly into the living room. A trip to the zoo, ho-hum before kids, takes on the thrill of an African safari. Children increase our capacity for joy.

Children, I believe, are also one of the best cures for the selfishness that plagues us, a firm answer to the question, "Could I really give up my LIFE for someone else?" Our unconditional love for them somehow lifts us up where we belong as human beings. Gives us glimpses of angel love.

But let's not get overly sentimental: parenthood also can turn a calm woman into a raving maniac, emotionally undone by the Chinese torture of sleeplessness or the siren-song whine of a toddler.

Recently I received a story about two girlfriends sitting at lunch. One of them, a certified mom; the other, just browsing at motherhood from her secure place on the career side of womanhood's window. As the mother struggled to explain what would happen should her friend toss out the birth control pills and buy pregnancy tests, her thoughts spoke for veteran mommies, worldwide:

I want to tell her what she'll never learn in childbirth classes: that the physical wounds of childbearing will heal, but becoming a mother will leave her with an emotional wound so raw she'll forever be vulnerable.

I could warn her that she'll never again read a newspaper without asking, "What if that had been MY child?"

I look at her carefully manicured nails and stylish suit and think that no matter how sophisticated she is, becoming a mother will reduce her to the primitive level of a bear protecting her cub.

I feel I should warn her that no matter how many years she's invested in her career, she will be professionally derailed by motherhood. One day she'll be going into an important business meeting and she'll think of her baby's sweet smell.

Looking at my attractive friend, I want to assure her that eventually she'll shed the pounds of pregnancy, but she'll never feel the same about herself; that her life, now so important, will be of less value to her once she has a child.

That she'll begin to hope for more years—not to accomplish her own dreams, but to watch her children accomplish theirs.

I want to describe to my friend the exhilaration of seeing your child learn to ride a bike. I want to capture for her the belly laugh of a baby who's touching the soft fur of a dog or cat for the first time. I want her to taste the joy that's so real, it actually hurts.

My friend's quizzical look makes me realize that tears have formed in my eyes.

"You'll never regret it," I finally say.

And that is exactly, though perhaps not as eloquently, what I finally told Heather—adding that it's a decision defying all rationality. She'd just have to close her eyes, hold her nose, and jump in. The water would be fine as soon as the initial shock wore off.

Six years after our last "Should we or shouldn't we?" conversation, we vacationed at the beach with Dean and Heather. Things had definitely changed, all around. There were few moments of serenity and pondering about life around a table of gourmet meals. In fact, I'm not sure if there was a single moment of relaxed chatting, and meals were of the microwavable-only variety. However, there was plenty of laughter and frustration and noise and mess and the kind of joy only young children can bring to a vacation at the beach.

As Dean, Heather, Scott, and I descended the wooden steps to try a stroll on the beach, we passed by a miniature polka-dotted swimsuit with hot pink ruffles, hung daintily over the rail. The little owner of the swimsuit soon interrupted our walk, chatting excitedly and pointing to a bucketful of squirming sand crabs. Her little brother, in navy trunks the size of a postcard, toddled along behind us echoing his big sister's sentiments, punctuating his talk of "cwazy sand cwabs" with an occasional squeal of pure delight.

We paused and turned and oohed and aahed at the treasures Nicole and little Scotty (named after my Scott) had gleaned from the sea. Heather bent down to shake some loose sand from Scotty's towhead, and gave Nicole a hug around her tanned shoulders.

"Do you ever regret it?" I asked, looking over at Heather and giving her a wink.

"Never," she answered. I looked in this mother's eyes as she stood, a sea breeze tousling her hair, obviously awed at the creation of her own offspring—and I knew I needn't have asked.

Don't you see that children are God's best gift?

PSALM 127:3 THE MESSAGE

To understand a parent's love: Have a child.
—**Japanese proverb**

The Girl I Used to Be

She came tonight as I sat alone,
The girl I used to be.

And she gazed at me with her earnest eye
And questioned reproachfully.

"Have you forgotten the many plans
And hopes that I had for you?

"The great career, the splendid fame,
All the wonderful things to do?
"Where is the mansion of stately height
With all of its gardens rare?

"The silken robes that I dreamed for you
And the jewels in your hair?"

And as she spoke, I was very sad
For I wanted her pleased with me...
This slender girl that I used to be.

So gently rising, I took her hand,
And guided her up the stairs
Where peacefully sleeping, my babies lay
So innocent, sweet, and fair.

I told her that these are my only gems,
And Precious they are to me.
That silken robe is my Motherhood
Of costly simplicity.

And my mansion of stately height is love,
And the only career I know,
Is serving each day in these
sheltered walls
For the dear ones who come and go.

And as I spoke to my shadowy guest,
She smiled through her tears at me
And I saw the woman I am now...
Pleased I'm the girl I used to be.

~ Author Unknown ~
From a wonderful website dedicated to mothers.
It even has music to ponder by!
http://members.aol.com/mempenny/mothers.html

2

The Pregnant Pause

I wrote the following as a fictional tale, but perhaps you'll see some of yourself in Lilly. I certainly did.

First Pregnancy

Month One:

She can't believe it. Lilly stares at the test results and holds them up to the cardboard box again and again, lining up the colors to make sure the matching hues mean "Yes, you're absolutely, positively, most assuredly, with child." Though she can't feel or see her new occupant, she struggles to accept that she's no longer a single-bodied unit. She's now, in fact, a duplex.

A baby, a thimble-sized miracle, who looks amazingly like a pinto bean, has boarded her body for a nine-month-long ride. Standing in the grocery store line, Lilly has to restrain herself from asking strangers if they haven't noticed her glow.

How could others not see the amazing transformation in who she's become—literally, overnight? Lilly's no longer just a woman, wife, student, or co-worker. She's joined the Society of Life Givers. The enormity of the thought fills her with unutterable joy, makes her want to waltz with the mailman, makes her… makes her… want to… throw up. Which she does. Morning after morning after morning.

Month Two:

Six weeks of nausea has put a wee strain on her unutterable joy. Lilly struggles to remember why she jumped so blithely into this motherhood pool and is tempted, more than once, to choke her husband, Will, who landed her there. How could anything, however noble, be worth emptying her stomach contents every hour on the hour?

She passes by a mirror and wishes, desperately, that she had not. How did she come to look so much like Granny Clampett in such a short time? Sleep—she must get more sleep. Sixteen hours of dozing per day is simply not doing the job.

Month Three:

At last, Lilly can see it coming—(drumroll please) The Happy Trimester! Well, it's about time. Things are lookin' up, stayin' down, and she, happy little momma, is goin' shopping for maternity clothes. Once at the Mother Knows Best Boutique, she tries on several tent-sized jumpers which all make her look like a large replica of Shirley Temple. She nearly snorts, she laughs so hard at the way the maternity pants fit around her barely-expanding waist. The enormous sags of excess material hanging down in front give her an oh-so-chic kangaroo look. But hey, who cares? She's in the Hoppity Happy Trimester.

Lilly pins up the pants with diaper pins (previously purchased at You're My Baby). Then she tosses a hot pink "Baby Hut" T-shirt over the gathers, pays for her new ensemble, and heads out to eat Italian food with the girls. Magnifico!

On the way home from lunch, she loosens the diaper pins to give her tummy a little more room for the baby and the lasagna and manicotti and ravioli and spaghetti with meatballs and oh, heavens, the spumoni.

"Gratzi, Señore, for all things bright and beautiful and smothered with mozzarella," Lilly prays with a staccato Italian accent. She finds, even now, alone in the car, that she can't stop smiling. Someone in the restaurant told her that she glowed, and fireworks of joy went off in her soul.

Month Four:

Today, when the house was still, she sat down on the living room couch and casually picked up a Jan Karon novel when something—no, *somebody*—fluttered. At first, Lilly thought, *No more meatballs for me,* but then she realized these were no ordinary tummy bubbles. These were baby bubbles! There's really a somebody doing aerobics inside the gymnasium of her womb.

She aches to see what her offspring looks like, what her baby is growing today. Is he getting big ears or curly red hair or a crooked little pinkie? She feels like the Willie Wonka Pregnancy Factory with marvelous, secret things brewing and stirring and being created inside. The desire to see the finished product seems almost too suspenseful to bear.

The ultrasound gives the pregnant couple a blurred black and white peek at their baby girl.

"It's a girl?" Lilly cries.

"It's a GIRL!" Will answers, stooping first to kiss the belly encasing his daughter and then his wife's forehead. Lilly tells the nurse that her baby girl will wear adorable lace anklets and Mary Janes and pink bows and bonnets and pinafores and all the ruffly, itchy, lovely things she flatly refused to wear as a young child.

What will we call this dainty daughter of ours? she wonders quietly, rubbing the outer-skin shell of her baby's cocoon.

Month Five:

Today Lilly finished decorating the nursery. It's been an enormous job, creating the perfect world for Katie, or Breezy, or Abby Lee to wake up to and go nighty-night in. There are splashes of all her favorite bright colors on the mural near her crib. Her daughter will awaken each morning to a lemon-drop sun and cotton candy posies and fluffy white clouds against a sky of robin egg blue. With purple and orange butterflies thrown in for good measure. Realism will come all too soon—she'll give her child a good pollyanna start. All the painted animals, from the fat little rabbit to the slow, shy snail are smiling toward the crib, as if enchanted under the spell of the fairy princess baby-to-be.

Bending carefully to one side, Lilly swoops a teddy bear off the carpet with one hand, and pulls a soft, new blanket, dotted with pink rosebuds, out of a gift box with the other.

Throwing the blanket over the bear, she props it above the hump of her burgeoning belly, his button nose against her neck, then sinks into the big wicker rocker and...imagines.

Pat, pat, rock. Pat, pat, rock.

She sings all six verses of "Hush Little Baby" before she catches a glimpse of Will, in full grin, standing in the doorway.

He comes near for a "Honey I'm Home" kiss, then eyes the bundled-up bear. "Don't worry, I won't say a word to the directors of the insane asylum."

"Good," she sing-songs softly, dreamily. "Then momma might buy you a mockin' bird."

Month Six:

Lilly removes the last pin from her once-baggy maternity pants. It makes a tinny sound as she lets it drop into the pink plastic cup labeled "Pins 'n' Things" The once-ridiculously droopy drawers now fit quite well. In fact, they're a bit snug. *Abby Lee or Breezy had better be a butterball of a baby*, she thinks, *or I'll be dining on a post-partum diet of Slim Fast and celery.*

Today Lilly cried. Just sat down and boo-hooed like a baby. Maybe, she reasons, mothers do some of the crying for their babies while the little humans can't make noises on their own, underwater as they are and all.

Why, when there are so many good things to look forward to, when having a baby is such a blessing from God, does she find herself crying?

Because she's wondering how, if the baby keeps growing at such a fast pace, for Pete's sake, will the little bitty opening in her body ever accommodate the passage of a seven-pound infant? The logistics, let's face it, seem preposterous. She remembers an old Carol Burnett bit where Carol, in top Yiddish form, says, "You wanna know what it feels like to have a baby? Take ya upper lip between ya thumb and ya forefinger. Good. Now pull it over ya head." She winces at the thought.

She cries because she wonders if she'll ever wear a belt again that doesn't make her look like jolly ol' Saint Nick.

She cries because her feet are disappearing beneath her, every day she sees a little less of her shoes. When she walks, it feels exactly as though she swallowed a bowling ball. Somehow she thought being pregnant would feel like having a tummy full of cotton or a helium balloon. She didn't anticipate this interminable heaviness. If only she could hand over her stomach to someone else to carry now and again. Just a breather.

She cries because she can't waddle three feet without having to go to the bathroom.

Sometimes Lilly wants to curl up in the nursery crib and suck her thumb until she falls asleep and the incubation is over. But if she did fall asleep, the baby would begin her Jazzercise routine.

Month Seven:

Finally, they settle on a name. Breezy it is. They both like the way it trips off the tongue, southern style. Lilly and Will looked for a name that would sound sweet, even as it was called out the back door, and over the front porch. "Breeeeeeeeeeeeeee-zy! Time to put away your mud pies and come in for supper!" Even when she's a teenager, they think, this is a name that should work just fine. "I'm sorry, young man, but Miss Breezy, our Breezy, you see, will not be courtin' until she's at least thirty-five."

Lilly can see the end of her pregnancy approaching on the month-by-month calendar with the pictures of upside down babies in wombs. But to her, in reality, the days ahead loom like an eternity.

Sometimes she worries that every other mother in the world will have their babies in nine months, but she'll be the one rare exception and—like the elephant she feels she is—remain pregnant for two years.

In fact, her ankles have swollen to match the width of her calves, giving a rather pachyderm effect.

She no longer walks—she lumbers, sways, and lurches.

All that's lacking, Lilly pouts, *is a trunk and tail.*

She can no longer reach the kitchen sink unless she washes the dishes by sitting sidesaddle on a stool pulled up to the counter. When she drives a car, Lilly feels like a toddler straining to reach the wheel and the peddles of her brother's Big Wheel. Or like one of those television Fruits of the Loom, with big-apple middles and stick arms and legs.

She tries reading funny books to keep from crying herself into a tizzy. Peering into the crib at the teddy-bear-in-a-blanket helps pull her out of the pre-baby blues, as does watching a little hump of a heel slowly careen across her belly.

Month Eight:

And holding.

Holding on to her heavy burden. Everything, from her breasts to her pelvic floor, feels as though it could fall down any minute. All of it—glands, bones, baby, skin—come crashing to the floor in a heap. *Why hasn't someone invented a pulley and sling*, Lilly wonders, *attached from the ceiling perhaps, or one of those IV bars on wheels, that I can use to help carry this load?*

Still, she holds on. To the side of the bed in a gargantuan effort to turn over, to stair rails and backs of furniture—anything to steady her uneasy gait.

But mostly she tries to hold on to her sanity.

Some days she manages fairly well, some days, not so good.

I will be pregnant forever, I'm sure of it, Lilly thinks. She tells God that if this is a test to see if she can be cheerful under the constant pressure and pain, she's failed it. She asks Him to give her a "D" and move on to another test.

Month Nine:

What do you know?

It happened!

It wasn't easy, in fact it hurt so absurdly much that Lilly longed, for the first time ever, to have an out-of-body experience. *God, please send me to Cleveland, for just a few hours,* she prayed. *Then put me back in this body when the baby has hatched.*

And then …. then came Breezy.

Sputtering and coughing and finally, blessedly, crying loud and strong and full.

She didn't know her baby's cries would pull so deeply at her heart that she'd actually feel the tug.

"Come here," Lilly coos, her arms outstretched to the miracle child.

"Here she is," says Will, his voice breaking as he hands her the infant, warm and wet and moving in slow motion just like a Thumbelina doll.

They stare, wordless in their wonder. The new father breaks the silence by saying, "You know, I want to buy her something very special for her birth day."

"A pink lace bonnet?" Lilly asks

"No," he smiles, "I was wondering, actually, if you knew where I could get a good buy on mockingbirds?"

You know exactly how I was made, bit by bit, how I was sculpted from nothing into something. Like an open book, you watched me grow from conception to birth …. The days of my life all prepared before I'd even lived one day.

PSALM 139:15,16 THE MESSAGE

The only time a woman wishes she were a year older is when she's expecting a baby.

Paul the Apostle, on Incubation & Waiting

Waiting does not diminish us, any more than waiting diminishes a pregnant mother. We are enlarged in the waiting. We, of course, don't see what is enlarging us. But the longer we wait, the larger we become, and the more joyful our expectancy.

Meanwhile, the moment we get tired in the waiting, God's Spirit is right alongside helping us along. If we don't know how or what to pray, it doesn't matter. He does our praying in and for us, making prayer out of our wordless, sighs, our aching groans. He knows us far better than we know ourselves, knows our pregnant condition, and keeps us present before God. That's why we can be sure that every detail in our lives of love for God is worked into something good.

Romans 8:24-28, The Message

3

Heavy Labor Day

May I speak with Becky Freeman?"

"Yes," I answered on the portable phone, shoving Daisy the barking dog out the door as I spoke.

"Becky, this is Vicki Crumpton. I was one of the editors invited to speak at the Southwest Christian Writer's Conference in Dallas. You and your mom were in my class, and you two asked if there was any interest in family humor in the Christian market."

My heart climbed past my throat and entered my eyeballs. I could feel them beating. *An editor! A real live book editor? Calling ME??*

"Well," continued Vicki, "I read one of your chapters—the one about your giving birth—to our publishing committee today."

I gave birth to a publishing committee? I thought for a split second, before getting my fast-spinning mental wheels back on track.

"Once we stopped laughing," Vicki chuckled as she spoke, "we decided that, yes, there is indeed a place for humor. We'd love to have your book in our spring lineup."

And that was how it all began.

Seven years ago, with the encouragement and help of my writing mother, I was typing our crazy family stories from a small spot in our cabin closet. And now, years later, my mother is still encouraging me—though mostly through her words and prayers, as she's backed away from full-time writing to more fully embrace other joys. Like homemaking, decorating, nutrition, exercise, gardening, dancing, church activities, and nurturing friendships. (I don't think I've ever seen my mother experience even a moment of boredom. As she joyfully flits from planting flowers to basting a roast, I've often heard Daddy say, "I like my women a little on the spunky side.")

Over the years, the Freeman Fam has finally built a semi-real house around and over our original cabin. (Stay tuned for the rest of that story in another chapter.) I've authored or co-authored almost a dozen books. The one thing that hasn't changed is that our crazy family tales keep coming, one after another. It's like the Old Testament story of the widow's pot of oil that won't run dry. Day after day, year after year, God grants bizarre story manna for my books and speeches.

For old time's sake, though, I thought it might be fun to re-share the story from *Worms in My Tea* that birthed it all. The tale that launched a fulfilling writing career and marked my unconventional debut into the wild wacky world of motherhood.

●●●●○

Back in the late seventies, the watchword of young and idealistic mothers-to-be was "Back to Nature!" Lamaze was the only way to go. I would one-up them—I would give birth in the warmth and intimacy of our own home. No conventional doctor, antiseptic hospital, or pain-blocking drugs for me, no siree.

On a Saturday morning in early December, I began to experience signs that this might be The Day. We notified our male midwife, and he promptly appeared at our door, did a quick exam, and agreed with our diagnosis. However, he said there was no rush to boil water or tear up a sheet for white rags. It would be a little while yet. He sounded lighthearted and wonderfully reassuring, and when we asked about going out to buy a Christmas tree to decorate in order to pass the time, he thought it was a jolly idea.

We notified our folks, and before they could throw down the phone and jump in the car, we told them it might be as long as six or seven hours. "No rush."

That evening, ten hours later, Mother served barbecue to us and the midwife and his red-haired female assistant. (No need to worry about nausea, since I definitely wouldn't be having any anesthetic.) Not much progress had been made other than a nicely decorated Christmas tree, but we were all still smiling and in a companionable mood. The lights of the tree blinked gaily into deepening twilight. The midwife, dressed in a T-shirt and jeans, told us during supper that he was a former Marine sergeant.

After supper, he announced that I needed to get busy walking to speed things up. At 2:00 the next morning, Scott was literally walking me through the house, standing behind me, holding me up and moving my feet with his feet. Mother was chewing her lower lip and glancing at the back bedroom, where sounds of the midwife's snoring issued forth, making her nervous. He was confident we were in good hands with his assistant, but at 3:00 A.M., Mother decisively made her move. We called out the Marine.

We'd figured things had to get tougher before they got easier, but when Mr. Midwife speeded things up, none of us was prepared for three hours of pushing. If I declined to push, the ex-Marine barked at me until I discovered there was one more push left in me after all. Scott's mother had dropped by for coffee 18 hours earlier, and still had enough wits about her to photograph the proceedings. My own mother was gyrating between moments of deep prayer on her knees in the kitchen and bawling idiocy.

As for the prospective mother, I'd have cheerfully strangled every natural childbirth expert who'd ever told me labor was not painful, just hard work. This was PAIN.

Scott supported my head and shoulders and coached, "Just think, the baby's almost here!"

"Just think," I shot back, "If I get out of this alive, you're going to be living a celibate life!"

At 6:30 that morning, 21 hours after we'd so blithely welcomed the first signs of impending birth, the midwife laid my 9 lb. 2 oz. son in my arms. Maybe the fact that I'm five feet two and small boned accounts for Zach's taking his good old time arriving, but it suddenly was all worth it. So much so, we managed to keep having them. And having them.

The birth of Baby Number Two seemed like a piece of cake compared to Baby Number One. Zeke arrived at mid-morning on a rainy June day, assisted into the world by a highly competent midwife and her two assistants. (As an aside, I might mention that the Marine had made the front page of our metropolitan newspaper, having been arrested. I'm not making this up.)

Baby Number Three would have none of making her appearance on a warm summer morning, but chose to make her debut three days after Christmas in 1983, one of the coldest winters in the history of the United States. Condensation froze on windows inside the house. My parents and my sister, Rachel, 18 at the time, were visiting for the holidays, and they all needed to return home. I was overdue and felt like a watched pot waiting to boil. I'd already "imagined" several instances of labor pains about which we'd notified our female midwife (a good friend by this time), but so far, I'd been unable to produce another grandbaby and a niece/nephew for my audience. But at about two in the morning on December 28, I woke Scott to tell him I was in labor.

"Go back to sleep," he yawned. "I don't even think you're pregnant anymore." The interesting thing is, I managed to fall asleep again, but when I next woke up, there was absolutely no doubt. I was pregnant, but I wouldn't be for long.

The scene that followed was like a choppy "Keystone Cops" episode. I yelled orders while Scott scrounged in the closet for the box of supplies I'd assembled for use by the midwife. I realized the box was now a "Do-It-Yourself Birth Kit" because the midwife was 30 minutes away in good weather. So much for the LaBoyer method I'd wanted to try.

Daddy got on the phone to the midwife and relayed messages to Mother, who hollered them to Scott, who was the most qualified at this point to officiate since he'd assisted at the first two home births we'd hosted. In the meantime, my very-together sister took careful notes in the section of her loose-leaf organizer titled "Things I Must Never Do," then dove in like a trooper, ready to boil water or tear up sheets, though we never figured out what we should have needed either for.

When the baby landed into Scott's waiting arms, he tearfully announced it was another baby boy. A few seconds later, Mother said, "Scott ... um.... I think you were looking at the umbilical cord there." We named her Rachel Praise, meaning "God's Lamb of Praise."

The midwife arrived in time to cut the cord, and Scott, now full of pride and self confidence, allowed as how he might offer a free baby delivery with each new home he built thereafter.

Three years later, Gabe arrived, and the birth happened so swiftly and smoothly that my mother didn't make it in time for the actual event, to her everlasting gratitude. During my recovery, she managed the three older kids and our household just fine, but Gabe was a little hard on her back. He weighed in at 10 lbs. 2 oz. Talk about your grand finale.

On the first day of February 1992, my sister, Rachel, gave birth to her fist child—her way. She went into labor, after a full night's rest, at about seven in the morning on her day off. Seven-and-a-half hours later, she called me from the hospital's exquisitely beautiful and homelike birthing room to tell me in graphic detail of the two painful contractions she'd endured before calling for the epidural.

"After that," she reported enthusiastically, "it was great. We all sat around and laughed and played gin rummy." That evening when I called to check on her and her new son, she could hardly talk because she was chewing steak from the candlelight dinner the hospital had served her and her husband (also a "Scott"). She apologized for cutting me short, but she had to call the gym before it closed and make her next racquetball appointment.

Good grief! I mentally ground my teeth. *She's managed a yuppie childbirth!*

As memories of my totally natural Lamaze, LaBoyer, LaLudicrous births swept over me, all I could think was, *What was I thinking?*

Seven years later, I still laugh at the differences between my sister, Rachel, and me. As might be expected, her son, Trevor, turned out a lot like Mary Poppins—practically perfect in every way. "May I please have some orange juice, Aunt Becky?" he asks nicely, as he sits, hands folded in quiet expectation, at my kitchen counter. When I bring the juice, he reaches up with a polite, "Thank you very much." I pat his head wistfully.

Having just finished a couple of unsettling interchanges with two of my own teenagers—in their sassiest form—I looked over at my sister and whimpered, "God loves you best."

As we broke out in laughter, she quickly reminded me that my children are unique and began reciting all my good qualities. Qualities she's sure my teens will appreciate before I enter menopause. Or at least before I qualify for free coffee at MacDonald's.

So even though Rachel jogs every morning, experienced a quick, near-painless childbirth, and produced a son that looks like a Precious Moments figurine—and even though she owns furniture that doesn't stick to the seat of her guests' pants, I have to admit I sure do love her.

She's my best friend and comforting kin, as we laugh and cry and pray and hang on to each other for dear life during this exhilarating, rickety ride called Motherhood.

A woman giving birth to a child has pain because her time has come; but when her baby is born she forgets the anguish because of her joy that a child is born into the world.

JOHN 16:21

If it was going to be easy, it never would have started with something called "Labor."

How Parenthood Changes with Succeeding Babies

(from Parenting *magazine, February 1998)*

Your Clothes
1st Baby: You begin wearing maternity clothes as soon as your OB/GYN confirms your pregnancy.

2nd Baby: You wear your regular clothes for as long as possible.

3rd Baby: Your maternity clothes are your regular clothes.

The Baby's Name
1st Baby: You pore over baby name books and practice pronouncing and writing combinations of all your favorites.

2nd Baby: Someone has to name their kid after your great-aunt Mavis, right? It might as well be you.

3rd Baby: You open a name book, close your eyes, and see where your finger falls. Bimaldo? Perfect.

Preparing for the Birth
1st Baby: You practice your breathing religiously.

2nd Baby: You don't bother practicing because you remember that last time breathing didn't do a thing.

3rd Baby: You ask for an epidural in your eighth month.

Worries
1st Baby: At the first sign of distress—a whimper, a frown—you pick up the baby.

2nd Baby: You pick the baby up when her wails threaten to wake your firstborn.

3rd Baby: You teach your 3-year-old how to rewind the mechanical swing.

Activities
1st Baby: You take your infant to Baby Gymnastics, Baby Swing, and Baby Story Hour.

2nd Baby: You take your infant to Baby Gymnastics.

3rd Baby: You take your infant to the supermarket and the dry cleaner.

Going Out
1st Baby: The first time you leave your baby with a sitter, you call home five times.

2nd Baby: Just before you walk out the door, you remember to leave a number where you can be reached.

3rd Baby: You leave instructions for the sitter to call only if she sees blood.

At Home
1st Baby: You spend a good bit of every day just gazing at the baby.

2nd Baby: You spend a bit of every day watching to be sure your older child isn't squeezing, poking, or hitting the baby.

3rd Baby: You spend a little bit of every day hiding from the children.

4

Baby Boot Camp: Prep for Graduation Day

aby Number One was an active but easy baby. Zach's hair was dark, his black eyes shined, and his smile was as bright as the Christmas season during which he arrived. He was so handsome that strangers would pause in their holiday shopping to admire him and coo their praises his direction.

Then, a mere 18 months later, came Zeke. When Zeke was born, my mother said, "Oh, my, Becky, he's ...well... he's—long!" Zeke (or Zeekle as Zach called him) was adorable, but adorable in the way ET was adorable. Big imploring eyes, bald head, long skinny legs. Spider Monkey adorable. Scott's cowboy brother Uncle Kent took one look at his new nephew and said, "He looks like a little alien, don't he? Hello, there, lil' trekkie."

I'd assumed that because I'd given birth at home, nursed my babies, and was basically a good girl most of my life, all my children would be easygoing. I never dreamed a homebred, homebirthed, breastfed baby of mine would be vulnerable to the evils of colic. But vulnerable, he was.

Night after sleepless night, Scott and I would try to calm nine pounds of screaming baby, passing him back and forth like a hot potato neither of us could handle. I'd gather what optimism I could and begin the bedtime saga by taking Zeke outside to the porch swing (thankfully he was a summertime baby) and rock him under the stars. Zeke would mercifully put his crying on "pause" as long as I kept swinging, but if I so much as skipped a beat, he screamed in protest. After an hour or so of this, optimism drained from every fiber of my being, I'd usually give up and start crying too. ("If ya can't beat 'em—join 'em.") When I'd swung all I could swing, I'd hand ET over to Scott for an hour of Daddy Therapy—which involved lots of moving and patting and pouting (from both father and son).

One day, not long after Zeke's birth, I woke up to find toddler Zachary carefully patting my Mary Kay eyeshadow into the bedsheets where I lay. Zeke had already begun his A.M. screaming session—his daily demand to know why I'd forced him out of his nice cozy womb into the cold, cruel world. Life as a young mother of an 18-month-old child and a fussy newborn, I concluded, was barely worth living. I could no longer even go to the bathroom alone. The most simple household tasks took gargantuan effort.

I caught Scott's eye as he walked out the door for work one morning. "When you come home," I asked him, irritation dripping from every word, "would you like me to have the bed made, supper fixed, or my make-up on? Because there's no way I can fit in all three between a full schedule of diapering, nursing, wiping noses, and perpetual SWINGING!" He asked me how I'd like to do his job instead—roofing houses in 103° weather. But before I could jump up and find a hammer and a bundle of shingles, he'd darted out the door.

I pried the eyeshadow away from my budding artist as I picked up Zeke and began bouncing him on one shoulder in an effort to calm him. At this point, the phone rang. It was my mother. I did what every distraught daughter does when her mother calls. I sobbed. I whined. I wallowed in my endless misery.

"Becky," she said soothingly, "I know this is a hard time. And I know Zeke's been a difficult baby, but listen, Honey. I think the Lord spoke to me this morning. Not audibly, but to my heart. And He said, *Just you wait and watch. Zeke will be Becky's joy.*"

"Mother," I cried, "I don't know! But oh, how I pray you'll be right."

Yesterday our family, along with Zeke's lovely girlfriend, Amy, and Scott's parents, drove five hours to Zeke's college in San Marcos, Texas, to watch him participate in his first triathlon. Unfortunately, Zeke got the dates for the race mixed up and missed the triathlon by exactly 24 hours. (He inherited his father's athletic ability and his mother's absent-mindedness.) But typical of Zeke, he laughed it off and turned his attention toward making the most of having his family around for the day.

"Hey!" Zeke said with enthusiasm. "There's a German Folk Festival in town today. Let's check it out!"

Within a half hour, we were standing in line for our "Wurst Fest" tickets, surrounded by gray-mustached men in red-button vests, leather shorts, and suspenders—flanked by aged Heidi types. Fifteen-year-old Rachel had a few sarcastic remarks to make about this "Worst Fest" as she rolled her eyes in exasperation. Not exactly the outing to the outlet mall that she and Gabe had hoped for this crisp autumn afternoon.

Smells of sauerkraut, sausages, and strong ale filled the air. A nearby band of German musicians ceremoniously raised their accordions and as soon as the first strains of a folk song wafted our way, I turned toward Zeke. I knew this child would be game for any activity smacking of fun, giving nary a thought to embarrassment. (This, another trait he got from his mommy.) I held out my arms, he held out his. He'd never done a polka in his life, but with Zeke, NOW is always the best time to learn. I gave him a quick ONE-two-three start, and with verve that covered our lack of skill, we polk-a-stepped, polk-a-stepped, all over the courtyard—to the delight of the crowd, and mortification of his younger siblings.

If you look up the word "enthusiasm" in future dictionaries, I'm sure "Zeke Freeman" will be found next to it. Before he graduated from high school, he launched a Christian coffee house, went on numerous mission trips, and spent two summers leading adventure trips for younger teens. He backpacks, kayaks, canoes, skis, rock climbs, runs, swims, snorkels, and scubas. He cares deeply. He loves without reserve. He laughs easily. He studies hard, works hard, plays hard, and prays hard. His kindness follows him everywhere he goes and leaves its mark behind. From the "Most Tenderhearted" award in Kindergarten to "The Fighting Heart" football trophy, Zeke has exemplified generosity and courage throughout his young life.

I will forever treasure his high school graduation day. In a way, I felt I was also graduating—to being a mother of two adult sons. (Zach had graduated early, two years before.) As the song, "Will You Remember Me?" piped through the auditorium speakers, Zeke stood up in his red cap and gown, walked over to me, kissed me on the cheek, and handed me a bundle of wildflowers. (Probably charmed a kind old lady into letting him pick them from her front yard.) I couldn't help but smile at his feet—adorned in his beloved Tevas, rubber soled sandals. Then he held out his arms, and I held out mine in return. We didn't have to speak; we knew what to do. We danced all over that gym floor. As I peeked over my tall son's shoulder, I couldn't see a single dry eye. Soon I was blinking back my own tears.

Mingled with the whirling 'round and the music marking my son's move toward adulthood, I heard an echo of my mother's prophetic words, spoken 18 years earlier on a day when I wondered if I'd ever survive this child.

"Becky, he will be your joy."

I leaned back to take in the handsome face of my baby, his doe brown eyes, strong jaw outlined with a hint of stubble, a wide smile to melt any woman's heart. There are some moments meant to be savored and treasured. Such were the minutes that I waltzed across a gymnasium floor with my son, joy of my heart, a living blessing in worn-out sandals.

"I will remember you, will you remember me?" the song played on. *Oh, yes, my child. I will remember you. Oh, how I'll remember you.*

Before the music stopped, I relinquished my son to the arms of his beautiful, golden-haired "Amy-Girl," who'd been patiently waiting her turn in Zeke's arms, and observed the light in my son's eyes when they met. As I watched them dance away, independent and secure in whatever the future held, I knew I was seeing joy personified.

To mothers of wee ones who wonder if the day will ever come when the crying will stop, when they can casually ignore the diaper aisle at the grocery store, when their babies won't need them for every little thing—trust me, that time will come. Every minute you spent in baby boot camp will pay off, a thousandfold, on their graduation day—and yours.

And the child…grew in stature, and in favor both with the Lord and men.

1 SAMUEL 2:26 NKJV

Do any human beings ever realize life while they live it—every, every minute? Oh, what I think when I see my youngsters growing up, the precious moments of childhood racing by. How can I squeeze every last second of fun, excitement, and sweetness out of those strange little creatures who are ours for so short a time?

Emily, from Thornton Wilder's

OUR TOWN

Erma, We Had the Same Child!

On November 3, 1979, Erma Bombeck wrote about her child who "marched to a different drummer." I'm convinced we shared the same child.

Of her son, Erma wrote, "As a child he wandered away from home to see parades ... got his arm caught in a construction pipe ..."

Oh, my, how I can relate! I once walked out onto the front porch around mid-morning. There stood Zeke, very still, with a large bucket upside down on his head. I never asked why, he never explained. Knowing Zeke as well as I do, I'm left to assume it was simply to see what it felt like to stand for five minutes with an upside down bucket on your head.

Erma wrote how these rare, unpredictable children are not only "out of step with the world but, if there's a puddle or a pile in front of him ... (he) will step in it."

We have no photos of Zeke, from age five months to 18 years, without some sort of mud smear across some part of his body.

Erma's boy "lost his billfold in the Grand Canyon, but the trip back to look for it was 'worth it.'" Incredibly, Zeke's Lost & Found Billfold has been mailed to us by benevolent strangers from all over the country (always during some "adventure trip") no less than three times. But inevitably, while he called home bemoaning the loss, he was simultaneously describing the "awesome scenery" and wishing desperately that "ya'll could see it with me."

Erma's son "borrowed the car and, when the radiator boiled over, poured Orange Crush in it. But," she added, "he was contrite."

Zeke, too, apologized profusely when his car engine committed internal combustion suicide and burst into flames while his father was driving it. He explained to Scott (who, after hitchhiking to get help, was more than slightly singed and confused) that he "never realized how important oil could be."

"His mail consists of brochures from causes and needs all over the world," Erma continued, "I have never heard him say, 'I'm too busy to talk to you.' Never heard him complain, 'The world is rotten....'"

Zeke, too, is the original Bleeding Heart Optimist. Even though he no longer lives here, we get mail from missions, orphanages, and "I Have a Vision!" projects all over the world.

"He dreams impractical dreams," Bombeck admits about her child. "He tries the patience of Job." You can almost hear Erma's sigh as she finishes up her essay. "But with his childlike trust and his zest for living, who am I to say that the drummer he marches to will not take him to the stars?"

Bravo, Erma.

I expect to receive a package in the mail someday with an alien-penned note tucked inside explaining, "We found this billfold in an upside down bucket near the Big Dipper. We believe it may belong to your son, Zeke. We already checked with Erma's boy, who is marching toward the Milky Way, but he says it's not his."

Becky Freeman

5

Udderly Ridiculous

I put my diaper bag down on the floor beside me with a sigh. My newborn son, wrapped in a blanket as soft as blue sky, was sleepily nuzzling my neck. I prayed he'd hold off for just a few minutes more before he demanded I serve up his mid-morning snack of milk and schnookies.

Glancing around the living room full of new mommies, I immediately began to feel comforted. Clearly, I wasn't alone in my struggles adapting to mommyhood. Our eyes all drooped from lack of sleep, the fragrance of "Eau De Last Spit-Up" drifted from our shoulders, and the telltale mark of every nursing mother decorated our blouses: two wet coaster-shaped circles, marking the place where normal breasts once abided.

Since giving birth to a child, we'd all marveled at the twin watermelon-sized feeding bags that swelled from our respective chests. Almost overnight we'd gone from being shapely, attractive women to your basic herd of Jerseys, with parachute-sized bras drying over the shower curtain rods.

Now, all we had left were mammaries...er, *memories*... of our less-than-missile-sized busts.

So here at La Leche League, we weekly turned to each other for affirmation and reminders of why we were choosing to breastfeed our offspring. (Actually, to avoid having to shout over two sets of burgeoning busts, we stood side by side.) We were a support group of bushed, big-bosom buddies.

One new mother, with tears in her eyes, said, "Nobody told me that breastfeeding would be this painful. I have a basket of teething rings next to the nursing rocker—for me!"

"You, too?" I asked. "I have to use my Lamaze breathing just to get over the initial hook-up, that first agonizing shock of attaching baby to breast."

"I hear ya," another woman chimed in. "Not only does it hurt, I feel like an unattractive hybrid of Dolly Parton and Quasimoto—leaning forward from this ponderous 'mother load.' I've contemplated stealing a grocery cart so I can slide these things into the leg holes of the kid seat and strap 'em in."

Laughter exploded around the room, and a bomb of relief and empathy went off in every corner.

"The other morning," I chimed in, "I woke up so full of milk that when I turned over, a stream of breast milk arched across the bed and hit the window. 'Nice shot,' my husband deadpanned, 'Now see if you can hit that fly over there.'"

"What did you say to that romantic comment?"

"I told him he was being udderly ridiculous."

Again the laughter, and with it the atmosphere lightened some more. We were now, so to speak, milking our predicament for all it was worth.

"The worst part for me," a red-headed mother explained, "is that I used to be a corporate executive juggling employees and projects. At the end of a typical work day, I could flip open my day planner and check off a whole list of accomplished tasks. Now, when my husband comes home and asks me what I've done, I say something like, 'I made half of the bed, then nursed the baby. I combed half of my hair, then nursed the baby. I got half dressed, then nursed the baby. I made it through half the day, fell asleep in the rocker, nursing the baby. I've been reduced to a rocking human feeding tube.'"

"Oh," another mom broke the brief silence. "Has anyone else answered the door for a repairman after feeding the baby, not realizing your blouse was hanging open?"

Moans of embarrassment echoed in reply. Seemed we'd all found ourselves at one time or another, unwittingly overexposed.

"Then why," I asked incredulously, "are we DOING THIS?"

"Well...it's good for the baby," one mother reminded us, as she burped her infant and deftly handed her toddler a Tippy Cup in one swift motion.

"Nothing's as nutritious as mother's milk, you know," said a full-time mommy and former pediatric nurse.

"And it's more convenient than bottles and nipples and formula and stuff."

At this point in the conversation, I had to mentally check out. Baby Zach was beginning to wiggle and protest. Enough was enough. He'd chewed on my empty neckbone all he was going to chew without a food-based reward for his efforts. It was time for the real thing.

As I watched him hungrily, frantically, wiggle his downy head back and forth in a desperate search for the source of all comfort, the elixir of life, I couldn't restrain a smile. I held my breath as he latched on, dreading the initial sting of pain. But soon the pain ebbed, and mother's milk began to flow. Tiny hands, twin pieces of living art, reached toward me, squeezing and patting my skin as if in gratitude. Then snagging a strand of my dark hair, he twisted it round and round in complete fascination at what he had caught. Two ebony eyes searched for mine, caught my gaze, and held it.

I could see my face reflected in those dark baby pools.

And what I saw was unconditional love.

I saw a woman who'd been molded into the shape of a mother by nine pounds of silky soft flesh, by a human in miniature whose very existence depended on her. After a few frantic gulps, Zachary began to suckle with less desperation, heaving an occasional contented sigh. Joy, relief from hunger, supreme happiness at being held and loved—these were the gifts I gave to my baby. A chance to nurture new life, to discover it was possible to love someone more than I loved myself, and if called upon, to die for them—these were the gifts my baby gave me.

As I glanced up, I saw mother after mother put baby to breast, in a ritual of love as old as humankind. Though we complained of the inconveniences involved in caring for new life, grieved the losses of our once-firm figures, and whined about absence of visible productivity—in our hearts, we knew the truth.

Never in our lives would we ever do anything as profoundly important as this.

It's been 13 years since I held one of my own newborns. I've moved on from diapering and nursing babies to getting a college degree while in my early thirties. I taught school for a short while. (Okay—a very short while. I retired from teaching first grade after nine months of faithful service.) By the time you're reading this chapter, I'll have written or co-authored a dozen books, spoken to audiences of thousands. I've met important people, with amazing influence, in significant places. And you know what?

I've still never done anything as profoundly important as nourishing life, fresh from the hands of God.

And I never will.

You made Me trust while on My mother's breasts.
PSALM 22:9 NKJV

To have my baby take nourishment from my body, to see his eyes drift shut, to hear his purring contentment, is painfully exquisite. How many mothers spend their children's lives trying to satisfy their own urge to give and protect and be needed? Now is the time to give myself over to the cuddling and crooning, so that as his need diminishes I can loose my hold without regret.

—from "Diary of a New Mother"
by Judith Geissler,
REDBOOK, September 1972

6

THAT'S Entertainment

We were in a pretty little town surrounded by the autumn painted hills of Tennessee. The conference where I'd spoken was a sweet success. (Meaning God was near and dear and the laughter hearty and plentiful.) Scott and I stood around chatting with the pastor. The hour was late and we were tired—but not hang-dog tired, more like goofy-sleepy tired, where you're relieved that all went well, and the smallest thing seems hilarious. I don't remember what started the conversation in the empty sanctuary, only that at one point I found myself talking with the pastor about how funny kids can be. He'd just admitted he often felt like a kid himself, that he was, in fact, ADHD. Sure enough, even as we walked and spoke, I couldn't help noticing the sort of shuffle-hop-skip method he used to propel himself down the aisle.

"What sort of toys did you have as a kid that you wish they made for grown-ups?" I asked, since we were all in a rather playful, creative mood.

After some deep theological discussion over the issue, we agreed there should be an adult-sized Johnny Jump Up for adult stress relief. Rather than yelling at the kids or getting a headache, an executive could shed his tie and jacket, harness himself in his Johnny Jump Up and hoppity hop his frustrations away.

Scott and I recalled and related how cute and funny our babies looked when they did their boing-yoing-yoing dances in their Johnny Jump Ups. They'd begin by bouncing softly a couple of times, their baby tennis shoes barely leaving the floor. The Warm-Up.

Then at some point—we never knew when or why—they'd suddenly get this Evil Kneivel look in their eyes, lower their eyebrows, screw up their mouth, ball up their fists—and jump-jump-jump-JUMP like there was no tomorrow. Zach had this hilarious squeal—like someone had just goosed his gizzard, that would send us scrambling for the cassette recorder (this was pre-video days). We couldn't pay for entertainment this good. At least not when we were twenty-year-old parents going through college on a janitorial salary. Scott and I would be laid out on the floor, tickled, watching our little Mexican Jumping Bean of a baby frantically trying to outjump his highest record.

"Oh, man," the pastor laughed as he recalled his first Jumping Baby encounter. "I think we may have an award-winning video from the day we tried our youngest child in a Johnny Jump Up. We made the mistake of putting him in the jumper BEFORE we hung it up, with the video going. So first you just see this little guy in his sleeper pajamas being dragged across the carpet by what appears to be a pint-sized parachute. In the next scene, it's obvious we hung the Jump Up too low—the baby looks like Otis Lee from the Andy Griffith Show—his feet criss-crossed and his body reeling around like an intoxicated little man. Finally the camera closes in on the kid's face, and he's looking at us, obviously bored out of his baby gourd, lazily spinning around in this contraption that his parents can't figure out how to hang. As his head circles around...and around...and around, he looks as if he wants to moan, 'The things I go through for these people.'"

When you think about it, babies have always been great for cheap entertainment.

My father used to get tickled just watching an average baby eating a cracker. Inevitably a baby will turn the cracker on its side—like a rolling Ritz tire—and attempt to eat it vertically. With upper and lower lips flattened against the cracker, the baby drools and scraps away with its one tiny tooth, never thinking to hold the cracker flat for an easy bite. They enjoy a challenge.

Oh, the joys of babies and food products! Before Scott became a father himself, we dined with a young couple who gave their baby a teething biscuit and stationed the infant in a high chair next to Scott's elbow. I sat across from them both and had a clear view of the whole scene. First the baby sucked on the teething biscuit until the entire thing was covered in a nice, soggy coating of drool and flour. Then, as Scott tried desperately not to notice, the child proceeded to paint its cheeks, forehead, and hair with the concoction. Scott gulped hard and looked away. But the baby was not one to be selfish with his treat.

He took his little gummy teething stick and tapped, tapped, tapped it on Scott's white dress shirt, leaving little soggy tan patches of biscuit behind with each tap. At this point, Scott graciously excused himself from the table. Though our hosts couldn't see him as he returned from his visit to the restroom, still green around the gills from his dining ordeal, I could. I was biting my cheeks, trying hard not to laugh, though it was obvious Scott was in serious distress. He didn't want to hurt our hosts' feelings, but he wasn't sure he had the stomach for any more scenes involving dribbles and bits. He signaled to me in a secret husband/wife code which I took to mean, "Is the little urchin finished with his dip stick yet?" Unfortunately, we were both to discover, teething biscuits are forever. Even though the baby had happily gone on to coat his high chair, his bib, and his mother's sleeve with biscuit goop—the cracker itself had barely diminished in size. It's the bread that keeps on giving. I'm even wondering if perhaps the five loaves, of the Five-Loaves-and-Two-Fishes miracle, were teething biscuits.

Let's face it, kids are funny. Just the pure, raw sound of a baby's first giggle is so addictively amusing, parents will do absolutely ANYTHING—and I mean ANYTHING—to get the next baby chuckle fix. Executive Daddies will pant like a dog or flap like a chicken, squawking loudly if need be, to hear the music of their infant's laughter. Mothers will blow raspberries on their baby's belly—precariously close to the wet diaper line—to persuade their offspring to produce a low chortle. Whatever it takes. "When the first baby laughed for the first time," said the ever-young Peter Pan, "the laugh broke into a thousand pieces and they all went skipping about, and that was the beginning of fairies."

I think Peter may have been right.

Then our mouth was filled with laughter.

PSALM 126:2 NKJV

Unrelieved lamenting would be intolerable. So for every ten Jews beating their breasts, God designated one to be crazy and amuse the breast-beaters. By the time I was five I knew that I was that one.

—Mel Brooks

Children Are Weird

Most experiences don't turn out the way we'd planned. Parenting is one of them. Take Spencer's second Christmas. Some in the church gave him a Nativity set as a gift. He was particularly taken with the wise men, one of whom he used as table ware. Dipped Balthasar up to his ears in ketchup and licked him clean. My wife said, "Honey, don't dip the wise man in the ketchup."

There are many things we anticipate telling our children. Things like, "Because I said so, that's why!" and "Not in this house you won't!" and even "Don't put that in the toilet!" But we never imagined ourselves saying, "Don't dip the wise man in the ketchup!"

Philip Gulley
Front Porch Tales

Part II

Days of Whine & Noses

7

The Sandman Cometh (Eventually)

One way to know you're growing up is when you think of bedtime as a luxurious reward at the end of a long day, rather than an ominous cloud hovering over your day on parade. At least that's what I'd always assumed. Until last night, that is, when my mother and I were discussing my sister's amazing ability to fall asleep just leaning against a reasonably soft wall.

"When we took her to Europe as a teenager," Mom said, "she slept draped over suitcases, stretched out on benches, through air turbulence that had most everybody else looped over little white baggies. On the other hand, I hardly slept the whole trip. The truth is, I hate to go to bed."

"Really?" I asked, curious. It's amazing to me, after all these years there are still things I don't know about my mother.

About that time my dad strolled through the living room. "Yeah," he agreed. "There she stands, night after night, stomping her feet and yelling, 'But I don't wanna go to bed!'"

"It's just that there are so many things I want to DO!" Mother pouted in retort. "I lie there with my mind going 90 miles an hour about all the lovely things I have planned for the next day, and the same thing happens the next day when the sun goes down. I've run out of time!"

"I've tried everything I know to get her to go to bed without a fuss," Daddy explained. "I've even tried making the bedtime ritual fun. Now that we're in our sixties, there's a whole new routine from 'I wanna drink of water! I needa go potty!' Now I tell her (he lapsed into his best coaxing-a-toddler voice) 'Come on, Honey. It's drops, salve, and ointment time!'"

I can hardly wait.

As you can see, one constant in our family is a keen sense of the theatrical. However, I can not relate to my mother's fight against sleep. At the close of one of my typically crazy days, I'm delighted for a chance to slip into unconsciousness. Just give me a pillow, a book, and a soft cozy nook, and I'm in paradise. When I began loving bedtime, I can't exactly say. I do know that getting married and being allowed to climb into bed with a handsome man, to enjoy spooning and snuggling my body next to his, made for a generally happier end to my days. In fact, I appreciate having someone to curl up with so much that I really empathize with little kids having to sleep alone with no one to snuggle beside.

There's a story I love about a little boy. It occurred on a summer evening during a violent thunderstorm. His mother was tucking him into bed and was about to turn off the light when he asked with a tremor in his voice, "Mommy, will you sleep with me tonight?"

The mother smiled and gave him a reassuring hug. "I can't, dear," she said. "I have to sleep in Daddy's room."

A long silence was broken at last by his shaky little voice, "The big sissy."

This bedtime anecdote reminds me of a time when Zachary was small and we were trying to get him to sleep by himself. Out of empathy and pity, we'd allowed our kids to waddle into our room in the middle of the night when-ever they were lonely or afraid (or hungry, or thirsty, or bored, or…). But after we added a few more children to our brood, Scott and I realized we were feeling like newborns ourselves, with days and nights mixed up—awake all night and sleepwalking through the day. We were no longer sleeping through the night, we were EXPERIENCING it. Reduced to sleeping on mattress spaces the size of tea towels, we realized something would have to be done. Something involving getting the kids out of our bed before we went out of our minds.

The first night after our resolve, Zachary, age four, tod-dled into our room and began his automatic sleepclimb into our bed. Though I was groggy, I got up, took his hand, and led him back to his own room. Needless to say, Zach was not pleased with this new arrangement. I reached for a large stuffed bear and snuggled it next to Zach, tucking them both in under a quilt.

"There," I said soothingly. "You have a nice big Pooh bear to sleep with now."

Zach took one look at the bear, turned his puppy-brown eyes toward mine, and said, "I'd rather have a nice big mommy."

My sister, Rachel, related how a similar bedtime revelation occurred to her son, Trevor. She wrote me the following in a letter:

Dear Becky,

The other night, we were exhausted with our efforts to get Trev to stay in his bed. We'd bought him a Power Ranger bedspread and matching sheets, and given him all kinds of bedtime toys to play with, but no matter what we did he wouldn't stay put. Finally I asked, "What is WRONG with your bed?" Trevor looked at us like...duh, we should KNOW what's wrong with it. Holding both hands toward the empty bed in exasperation he said, "There's no people in it!"

Thankfully, our lastborn child, Gabriel, was surpassingly easy to put to bed even as a little guy. At first, I thought this ease into bedtime might be because he could bunk with a big brother, which kept him from feeling too alone. But then one night I discovered Gabe had an unusual, secret, and active nightlife. As I sat by his bed before tucking him in, he confessed the whole thing. "See," he explained carefully, "when everybody in the house is asleep, I go in their rooms and get good stuff from under their beds."

"Like WHAT?" I asked and then, without thinking, asked if he wasn't afraid to go roaming around the house after dark, sticking his hand under beds. Gabe looked at me as if I'd lost my mind.

"Are you kidding? NO! You can get some really good stuff!" As proof, Gabe reached behind his own bed where he'd been keeping his stash from these nocturnal missions.

With a grin that grew as he took out each item, he displayed a tennis ball, a pile of rubber bands, an old piece of candy, and a "Jake's Good n' Plenty Bar-B-Que" Frisbee.

So while we were having sweet dreams, Gabe was going huntin' after midnight, stalking the floor under us. (Why do I feel like I just wrote a line from three country songs?)

But back to my original musing. When did I start to love, even savor, going to bed? I think it occurred when the children grew older, and the nighttime ordeal became mercifully less traumatic. When they were tiny, we had such an involved bedtime routine. I read to them, bathed them, rocked them, sang to them, prayed with them, nursed or watered them, diapered or pottied them, bear hugged them, kissed them, and stopped often to gaze at them—cute as a basket of baby bunnies in pastel feety pajamas. Then I repeated many of these things several more times throughout the evening before they actually fell asleep. By that time, I was wiped out—too exhausted even to cry, much less marvel over how cute they were.

To this day, I'm grateful for teenagers who come find me to say their goodnights, who bathe themselves, nurse their own drinks of water, and turn out their own lights. Who often, *voluntarily*, go to bed before I do, leaving me the quiet gift of an unhurried evening before I drift off to sleep.

As a matter of fact (pardon me while I yawn), it's getting pretty late and my eyelids are drooping. Won't you join me in a sleepytime hot chocolate toast to bedtime? Cheers to the best little snorehouses in Texas (and elsewhere). Hold tight your blankie, grabbeth thy storybook, and snuggle up to your favorite nighty-night pal—be he stuffed with fluff, or snoring softly and filled with love.

Yes, you will lie down and your sleep will be sweet.

PROVERBS 3:24 NKJV

Small children disturb your sleep, big children your life.
—**Yiddish Proverb**

Random Thoughts from a Tired New Father

I've been a father for about two weeks now and my son Malcolm is great, although his first week, he did get out of line. Messy diapers and crying about everything.... He's such a baby.

Sleep deprivation is the order of the day as Malcolm dictates the pattern of slumber.... I will say, however, that last night I slept like a baby.

I cried all night and wet the bed.

Robert Byron
Parents Say the Darndest Things

8

Life in Slow Motion

Do you remember the famous Tim Conway skit—the one where he plays the old man with Einstein hair, who shuffles along at the speed of a wounded snail? The skit varies, but the outcome is always the same—he drives fellow actor Harvey Korman insane, his nerves worn to the nubs by the old man's earnest, but barely perceptible, efforts at moving or doctoring or repairing.

Well, I ran into The Cracker Barrel yesterday to get a few Christmas presents and on the way out found myself ground to a near halt by a herd of Mr. and Mrs. Scoot-Along Conways enjoying an outing with their senior adult Sunday school class. Though I love elderly people, I was in a big hurry and found my forbearance in short supply. By the time the group had inched their way from the door down the steps to the parking lot, I'd overheard which Beanie Babies were purchased for assorted grandchildren, what each member had especially enjoyed for lunch, and the effect of such a lunch on a bevy of internal organs (all this accompanied by hand motions and special sound effects).

I finally found an escape hatch through the gang of shuffling seniors, and as I made a break for my car, it dawned on me that it had been a long time since I'd been forced to move at such a slothlike pace. The last time, in fact, that I'd been put in slow-motion confinement was when I took my last toddler on a trip to the mall.

A typical trip to the mall with a toddler should never be attempted by a woman with a schedule to keep. Why? Okay, you asked, so here goes.

The average toddler whines, cries, and moans in the car all the way to the shopping center, but once you finally, blessedly, pull up and park, he falls instantly asleep in his carseat. You then undo the numerous buckles of his carseat's harness, put the little guy in a stroller—careful not to let his sleepy head roll off to the side—and buckle copious doodads until baby is securely fastened on board this new deal on wheels.

By the time you reach the heavy glass doors of the shopping mall, Baby Houdini—who will have miraculously awakened and escaped the stroller's sixteen-point harness—is now standing up in the seat. He reaches lovingly toward some ominous teenager (sporting demonic tattoos and half a dozen piercings) and pleads, "Hold me!" as he leans out the stroller at a precipitous angle. Just before your toddler plunges toward a concrete concussion, you reach down and scoop him out of danger. Exhausted, you realize it's been 30 minutes since you parked the car, and you've not yet made it to the other side of the mall door.

I've lost track of how many times I found myself moving in zombielike fashion through the Child's Play store, my toddler leading me from Ugly Toy to Useless Toy in an "I Want

Dat!" frenzy. The stroller had been reduced to a decorative trailer for hauling the diaper bag, and I'd been reduced to a decorative appendage to the toddler, who long ago decided to take control of the situation.

Once, desperate for a break, I stopped at the food court to buy chicken nuggets to share between the baby and me (nourishment for the slow death march back to the car). But soon I discovered my child was already snacking on an appetizer of roach body parts, his tiny fingers having deftly pried them up from a crack in the table while I turned for the half second it took to open the dipping sauce. I offered him a sip of milk, hoping to dilute the bug toxins, which he spit across the table, spraying the back of the mall janitor's head—his cute little way of saying, "I wanted *Root Beer!*"

The best thing about having to take small children on errands is that you will ever after be grateful for life's small, speedier blessings. Oh, the bliss of simply grabbing your keys and a lightweight purse, and zip-zipping around town again. No buckles, no bags, no strollers to cramp your style or bog your step. Like the little, lisping, impassioned mouse from *American Tail*, you feel like shouting, "Fweedom! Fweedom! Let's have a rouw-y!" You're released from ever having to drag down endless rows of plastic toys: You may choose never to eat a pre-formed, lukewarm trapezoid of chicken again.

It occurs to me that we slowly toddle our way into the world, then somewhere along the way we pick up speed until we reach midlife and find ourselves practically racing through our days. Then, a few years later, when we're able to spy the "Exit Life" sign on the horizon, we put the breaks on and begin easin' up on the gas. We Sunday-drive as slowly as possible on our way out of this world. As Harold Munro said, "Here's a new day. O Pendulum move slowly!"

"What's the hurry?" both toddlers and the elderly—stationed at each of life's poles—seem to ask. "You might miss something interesting if you go too fast. Might pass up a cricket head, or a rainbow shimmering off an oil spot. Or a nice pea salad."

The only difference is that the elderly admonish us to "stop and smell the roses," while toddlers simply eat them.

Consider the lilies of the field, how they grow: they neither toil nor spin.

MATTHEW 6:28 NKJV

Hold every moment sacred.
Give each clarity and meaning,
each the weight of thine awareness, each
its true and due fulfillment.
—Thomas Mann

A Baking Recipe for Mothers

1. Preheat the oven. Check to be sure there are no rubber balls or plastic soldiers lurking on the racks.

2. Remove blocks and toy cars from table. Grease pan. Crack nuts.

3. Measure two cups flour. Remove Johnny's hands from the flour. Wash flour off him. Re-measure flour.

4. Crack more nuts to replace those that Johnny ate. Put flour, baking powder, and salt in sifter. Get dust pan and brush up pieces of bowl that Johnny knocked on the floor. Get another bowl.

5. Answer the doorbell. Return to kitchen. Remove Johnny's hands from the bowl again. Wash Johnny. Answer the phone. Return to kitchen.

6. Remove ½-inch salt from the greased pan. Look for Johnny. Grease another pan. Answer phone. Return to kitchen and find Johnny.

7. Take up greased pan and remove layer of nut shells in it. Head for Johnny who runs, knocking the bowl off the table.

8. Wash the kitchen floor, table, walls, and dishes.

9. Call the bakery and place an order. Take two aspirins and lie down. Don't forget to turn the oven off!

9

Germs of Endearment

Who in their right mind would willingly hold out their hand to accept donations of a half-chewed Tootsie Roll, a freshly blown tissue, or a wriggling worm?

Who rushes to comfort a child with a virus, knowing full well that as soon as she reaches that child, her robe will be wearing the remains of last night's pre-digested pizza?

Who finally succumbs to the unrelenting choruses of "Isn't he cute?" and "We'll promise to feed him," only to awake some sub-zero morning to the reality that the fur-that-followed-them-home is now her sole responsibility?

Who else but, of course, our mothers.

Robert Fulghum described the one person in his house that sent him into orbits of awe because "she could reach into the sink with her bare hands—BARE HANDS" and pick up the lethal gunk from the sink drain. To top that, he once saw her "reach into the wet garbage bag and fish around in there looking for a lost teaspoon BAREHANDED—a kind of mad courage. She found the spoon in a cup of coffee grounds mixed with scrambled egg remains and the end of the vegetable soup." Fulghum adds, "I almost passed out when she handed it to me to rinse off."

Without a doubt, we all know, this brave woman had to be none other than young Robert's mom.

Whose saliva can slick back the wildest curl, clean the toughest jelly stains from a five-year-old's cheek, and promptly cure infectious lesions?

Who can talk on the phone, fold a diaper with one hand, scold a child with one raised eyebrow, and elbow the front door closed while performing two sets of leg lifts?

Who runs in a panic when her toddler squeals to "See what I've done!" and breathes an enormous sigh of relief when she discovers the excitement is over a properly pooped-in potty.

Who calms all fears, cleans dirty ears, and though she grows weary, also grows more dear through the years?

Who exchanged the Days of Wine and Roses for Nights of Whines and Runny Noses?

No one else, of course, but our mothers.

With this impressive resumé behind our own mothers, what choice did we have when we reached grownuphood but to follow in her maternal house shoes, bear children, and become mothers as well? However, we found that parenthood was far from an instant success. It required education, experience, and multitudes of long-distance phone calls to Mother.

I recall three times in my life when I profoundly needed a mommy: when I was six and woke up with a bad dream; when the girls in fourth grade wouldn't play with me; and when I was 20 years old and left all alone with my firstborn child for the first time. Maternity loomed like eternity. I took one look at that fragile child sleeping blissfully in his crib,

unaware of the danger he was in, and realized with profound finality that he was wholly dependent on me for his
continued existence. I felt I at least owed him some explanation of the bind we were in and how I planned to get us
through it.

"Look kiddo," I whispered to Zach's sleeping form, "I
know I look awfully young and naive to be taking on this
Mommy Job. But hang in there. Don't move. Don't wake
up. Don't ANYBODY PANIC! I can call in a professional Real
Mommy if things start to get out of hand and I forget where
I leave you, or feed you a jar of cold cream instead of baby
food, or put toothpaste on your diaper rash."

Thankfully, my mother adapted to her role as Granny
with near euphoria and proceeded to show me how to feed
and bathe my little charge and, perhaps most importantly,
how to communicate in newbornese. This involved holding
the gazing baby with his head resting in the palm of my
right hand and, using a high-pitched voice, speaking in a
language that sounded one-third English, one-third Pig Latin,
and one-third Cajun. "How's our witzy, bitzy, baby boy doin'
dis mornin', huh? Dat's right, dat's right—you done blowed
a good wittle bubble-y with your moufy, didn't you?"

With my mother's expert coaching, I became a passably
good mother myself in a relatively short amount of time. I
didn't misplace my baby, I never mistook cold cream for
baby food, and only once did I accidentally mixup the toothpaste with diaper ointment. Scott still remembers the shock
of a mouth full of Desitin. ("But, admit it," I told him years
later, "you never had one oral outbreak of diaper rash, now,
did you?")

As my first baby grew and others arrived to keep him
company, I found myself mixing and mingling with other
mothers like the pro I'd become. Why, I could pack a diaper

bag in less than five seconds, make a peanut butter sand-wich so good it would halt a child in mid-whine. I could anticipate a toddler's runny "ker-choo!" with a ready tissue, and leap a pile of Legos with a single bound. (If you've never stepped on a Lego in the dark of night, well, let's just say one does learn how to leap.)

When I survived the month-long Invasion of the Chicken Pox, and at least 24 midnight "Mom-meee, I'm sick at my tummmmeeeeeeeee!" calls, I knew I had earned my mommy merit badge and could hold my own in any Play Group.

Now I'm 40 years old. How did that *happen?* In two short months, my firstborn son will be 20. (*That's* how it hap-pened. My child aged me). Zachary will be the same age that I was when I became his mother. Wow. It's so hard to believe. My baby, given the right circumstances—like a wife and a job—could have a baby of his own.

Currently, thankfully, Zach is single and still finding his way in this world. Marriage and babies seem a long way off in some far distant future, to him.

But today he dropped by for a brief visit and told me how he'd begun to enjoy a couple of his friends' little babies. How he loved holding them and jiggling them up and down until they giggled and burped. How soft their skin was and how trusting they were of the big people around them.

"Someday ..." he said with a far-off look in his eyes.

"Someday ..." I answered. "And, Zach, you'll be a won-derful father."

"Thanks, Mom," he replied, with a grateful grin.

I stood up, patted his shoulder, feeling peacefully serene in my roll as "Mom/Someday Granny."

Then I rolled up my sleeves, walked toward the kitchen, and as a silent gesture of gratitude to my own mother (alias

"Someday Great-Granny") resolutely fished the goop out of the drain, BAREHANDED.

Her children arise and call her blessed... Many women do noble things, but you surpass them all.

PROVERBS 31:28, 29

Parents do a lot of gross things in the name of motherhood and fatherhood. It doesn't matter on what economic level you live, when a child hands you a shoe with a knot in the shoestring that he has wet on all day long, the first thing you do instinctively is put it in your mouth and try to loosen up the knot with your teeth.
—**Erma Bombeck**

Real Mothers

Real Mothers don't eat quiche; they don't have time to make it.

Real Mothers know that their kitchen utensils are probably in the sandbox.

Real Mothers often have sticky floors, filthy ovens, and happy kids.

Real Mothers know that dried Play-Doh doesn't come out of shag carpet.

Real Mothers don't want to know what the vacuum just sucked up.

Real Mothers sometimes ask "Why me?" and get their answer when a little voice says, "Because I love you best."

Real Mothers know that a child's growth is not measured by height or years or grade. It's marked by the progression from "Mama" to "Mommy" to "Mother."

10

Kid's Eye View

ometimes, when addressing an audience of women, I'll explain what the word "humble" means to me. In particular, what it meant that Jesus "humbled Himself" for our sakes. The word comes from the Greek word "hummus" meaning "earth." It has the connotation of being brought down low.

"What do you do with your physical body when a child comes to your front door, or into your classroom," I ask aloud, "and you want to make an instant connection with him or her?"

All over the audience I hear women softly saying, "Scoot down low," or "Get on their level." Isn't that true? It's automatic. When God wanted to connect with human beings, He sent His Son to come down on our level, to meet us here on earth, face to face, eye to eye.

In the same way, to connect with a small child, we scoot down to their level. But more than that—we try to see life from their wee point of view. Yet even when we think we understand the inner workings of a child's mind, they still manage to throw us for a loop.

My mother loves telling about the day my daughter, then three, gave the following explanation for our moving to East Texas from where we once lived near Ft. Worth. "Baby Gabey had a real shooey diaper," Rachel told her granny, matter of factly. Then she sighed and concluded, "We had to move." In Rachel's pint-sized way of viewing the world, that dirty diaper was the last straw. We were left with no choice but to relocate 200 miles away from the unredeemable mess.

Another time, my mother was driving with Gabe in the front seat. He, too, was around three at the time. (I've always said that three-year-olds yield the most humor per square inch. I've been known, in a writing pinch, to borrow a friend's three-year-old for material.) The traffic was just horrible, cars darting in and out all trying to get out of the city. Gabe looked over at my mother and offered his best explanation for the chaos. "Gwanny," he drawled, "nobody knows where they leee-uve."

I love the story of the grandmother who was babysitting her young grandchild. As they sat coloring pictures the grandmother decided to sneak in a little education. She held up a crayon and asked her granddaughter, "What color is this?" The little girl obediently answered, "It's red." Then the grandmother picked up another color crayon and asked, "Now, can you tell me what this color is?" Again, the child answered correctly, "It's blue, Grandma." On and on this little scene played out until finally, in exasperation, the child responded, "Grandma, I really think you should figure out some of these for yourself!"

Children see the world quite differently, and even if you don't agree with their refreshing new viewpoint, you can at least enjoy some wonderful chuckles. A kid's-eye view I admire, untainted by the word's negativity, is their unbridled optimism. They tend to frame events in the best light, believing for the best possible outcome.

A couple of years ago I went to Colorado Springs to visit my good friend Lindsey O'Connor. (She's a fellow author and wrote the wonderful book, *If Mama Ain't Happy, Ain't Nobody Happy*.) Lindsey has four beautiful kids, who stairstep from Kindergarten Kid all the way to Driving a Car. The youngest is Allison and what a heartstealer she is. While I was in their home one night, I walked to the top of the stairs in the middle of the living room and tumbled, head over heels, down the entire flight of stairs.

I landed in a kind of sad heap at the bottom just in time to see Allison's pajama-feet. For a moment all was silent. She stared at me with puzzled interest; I was struggling to catch my breath. Finally, six-year-old Allie broke the silence by lying down, face up, on the carpet and folded up in a little ball, her feet extended over her head.

"Now," she said pleasantly, as she lay curled up, her face squished against her knee caps, "can you do THIS?"

Suddenly, I felt much, much better.

It reminded me of the optimism of the little boy whose Little League team was behind by 14 runs. When asked if he felt discouraged, the little guy cheerfully piped, "No way. We haven't been up to bat yet!"

Or the little girl trying out for a play. Her mother was worried her daughter wouldn't get a part, until her little one announced, with great enthusiasm, "I've been chosen to clap and cheer!"

The incredible way kids look at life through rainbow-colored lenses makes me want to crawl around on my knees some days, just to see the world they see.

Very young children have such confidence, too. Before we swipe it away in an effort to temper their pride, they believe the universe is theirs to embrace and comprehend. Nothing is beyond their scope. A precious little boy drew a picture in Sunday school. His chosen subject? God Almighty. Yes, he took on the Big One, decided to draw a picture of God. When his teacher discovered this, she gently said, "But, Honey, nobody knows what God looks like." Undaunted, the kid kept right on coloring, only pausing briefly to assure her, "They will when I get through with this."

On a recent trip to the hill country, my sister, Rachel, was telling me about a little boy, Dylan, who was very seriously trying to explain how the hierarchy worked in a popular superhero cartoon.

"Ms. Rachel," he stammered excitedly, "did you know that if the WHITE Ranger isn't there, then the GREEN Ranger is the leader, and if the GREEN Ranger isn't there, then the RED Ranger is the leader, and if the Red Ranger isn't there, then…then…" Dylan's eyes darted off to the side as he consulted his wavering memory, then with a sense of renewed authority, he announced, "Well, the Red Ranger just has to always be there."

In a child's mind, there's no provision for life without the Red Ranger. He HAS to exist or the cartoon kingdom is doomed to the unthinkable, the unfathomable.

In mulling over pint-sized thought processes, I've come to realize there are some pretty giant truths zipping around in their wee little noggins. And, as the little crayon-toting child said, we really should have figured out some of these things for ourselves by now. What lessons? How about…

1) *Moving On*, from Rachel: Sometimes you just have to cut your losses, admit the mess you've landed in is too big, and head on to something else.

2) *Profound Thinking*, from Gabe: Perhaps too many of us on life's busy freeway really have all forgotten where home is.

3) *Perseverance*, from Allie: Now that you've fallen and gotten embarrassment over with, can you get up and do something else wonderful?

4) *Optimism*, from the Little Leaguer: Hey, it ain't over until it's your turn to bat.

5) *Humility*, from the would-be actress: When you're chosen to participate from the audience side of life, accept the honor with gratitude—and clap and cheer for all you're worth.

6) *Theology,* from our little cartoon watchin' Dylan: It ain't even worth thinking about life without the Big Guy in Charge. There HAS to be an Ultimate Hero to fight evil forces, or this world is unthinkably doomed.

And if you don't know who that Hero is, I know another little boy who'd be delighted to draw you a picture of Him.

Out of the mouth of babes...You have ordained strength.

PSALM 8:2 NKJV

Pretty much all the honest truth-telling in the world is done by children.

—Oliver Wendell Holmes

Resignation from Adulthood

I am hereby officially tendering my resignation as an adult.

I have decided I would like to accept the responsibilities of an eight-year-old again.

I want to go to McDonald's and think that it's a four-star restaurant.

I want to sail sticks across a fresh mud puddle and make a sidewalk with rocks.

I want to think M&Ms are better than money because you can eat them.

I want to lie under a big oak tree and run a lemonade stand with my friends on a hot summer's day.

I want to return to a time when life was simple.

I want to think the world is fair. That everyone is honest and good. I want to believe that anything is possible.

I want to be oblivious to the complexities of life and be overly excited by the little things again.

I don't want my day to consist of computer crashes, mountains of paperwork, depressing news, how to survive more days in the month than there is money in the bank, doctor bills, gossip, illness, and loss of loved ones.

I want to believe in the power of smiles, hugs, a kind word, truth, justice, peace, dreams, the imagination, mankind, and making angels in the snow.

So... here's my checkbook and my car keys, my credit card bills and my 401K statements. I am officially resigning from adulthood. And if you want to discuss this further, you'll have to catch me first, cause...

"Tag! You're it."

11

Before There Was Barney: Child's Play in the Prehistoric Era

My sister, Rachel, her seven-year-old son, Trevor, and I had just watched my son, Gabe, run the ball for five—yes, FIVE!—touchdowns in the seventh-grade football game. Needless to say, by the time Gabe packed his sweaty, jerseyed frame into the front seat of the car, a spirit of celebration prevailed. Little Trev was near speechless with admiration, as Gabe reached over and tousled his cousin's brown hair. The only thing better than making five touchdowns in one game is having a little one-person groupie around to adore you.

"Hey, Gabe," my sister said, "I think this calls for ice cream."

Gabe grinned in agreement. Trevor chimed in, "Yeah, yeah, yeah!" This kid is always game for anything smacking of adventure—or sugar.

Within a few minutes I pulled my faded red van ("The Sun-dried Tomato," we call it) into the parking lot of a small-town Dairy Queen.

"Look, Trev," I said, noticing a fenced area next to the DQ, "there's even a playground for you!"

As we emerged from the van and walked toward the restaurant, it was soon evident that the designers who worked on this fast-food playland were minimalists. The floor of the playground was made of loose pebbles, and sticking up from the pebbles, like long sunflower stems, were four sticks with steering wheels attached to the ends. No pretend planes, trains, or automobiles here. Just rocks on the floor and four sticks with wheels—like steering-wheel lollipops.

"Gee," my urban-raised sister commented, "they really expect ya to use your imagination in the country, don't they?"

I stifled a laugh, but Rachel was on a roll, using her best hick imitation, her thumbs hooked in her belt loops. "Hey, Beck, I can just hear the playground architects saying, 'Listen now, don't spoil them kids. They don't need none of that fancy play 'quipment. Don't need no shiny slide or hoity-toity swing set. Just give 'em a stick with a steering wheel on it.'"

By now I was laughing out loud. We went inside the DQ and ordered chocolate-dip cones all around. While Trevor went out to make the most of the wheel-on-a-stick enter-tainment, I began to muse and ramble about my favorite childhood playthings.

"Rach, when I think back to all the toys we had when we were little—the Barbies and board games and badminton sets—I have to admit my favorite playthings were made of natural ingredients, not pre-formed plastic."

"Like what?"

"Well, I loved making mud pies, especially at Nonnie's house."

"Oh, yeah," Rachel remembered, "she had the best dirt— in lots of different colors, too."

"That West Texas red clay made the prettiest icing."

"And the colored pebbles were perfect for 'candy' decorations."

"Some of my favorite childhood memories were from Nonnie's backyard."

Rachel nodded. "Remember the baby horned toads? They were like tiny soft bodied dinosaurs. I thought they were neat then, but now I realize what an unusual play toy they really were. Did you know that they're endangered?"

"No! They were soooooooo cute! Nonnie used to keep her eyes peeled for them when she weeded the flower bed. One baby horned toad could keep us happy for hours. Probably gave Nonnie more free time to cook and clean than a pack of videos gives the average preschool mother today."

"Yeah, how did moms survive life before Barney?"

"They gave us dirt and water and sticks and a big back yard and told us to go play."

"They did, didn't they?"

I reflected back. And it wasn't a bad deal at all, as I recalled. There was something wondrous about creating a fort from old fallen trees, about building mud castles in the grass for doodlebugs and crickets. Summer evenings were spent running through sprinklers, playing "Mother, May I?" or catching lightnin' bugs (or "mosquitoes with flashlights") in a mayonnaise jar. When winter settled in, and we were forced to take our imaginations indoors, I kept myself enthralled many an afternoon making shoebox houses for my tiny dolls. I'd busily scrounge up thread spools for miniature stools and chairs, turn paper muffin pan liners into lamp shades, and set tiny tables with button dishes and thimble cups. The whole process of creating a tiny kingdom fascinated me.

Then, one birthday, my mother took an old bookcase and made it into a fancy dollhouse. She even sewed soft pink curtains and made a miniature bedspread and pillow trimmed with lace. At first I was delighted with its loveliness. Everything my mother had made was perfect and looked so professional, so neat and pretty. Then, surprising even myself, my heart sank as I realized I'd probably be expected to actually PLAY with the dollhouse—when what I really wanted to do, in my little heart of hearts, was to CREATE a Dolly Land of my own design. It wasn't the *product* I loved, it was the *process.*

Though I risk sounding like my own parents, life seemed somehow simpler when I was a child, before the invasion of malls and MTV. Television was there, but it was rarely on. We preferred playing with friends or playing games. When I turned about ten or eleven, Mother taught all the neighborhood kids how to play card games like Hearts and Spades. Kool-Aid flowed like a river that summer as we sat around the kitchen table, throwing fits of convulsive laughter whenever our mother got stuck with the wicked ol' Queen of Spades.

My mother also gave me the gift of "how-to." She taught me how to work a puzzle, play games, and bake from scratch. As soon as I was old enough to sift flour, I was allowed to bake whatever struck my fancy on Saturday afternoon. I loved blending together the raw ingredients of flour, sugar, eggs, cocoa, and butter into an edible work of art. I spent many weekday afternoons copying recipes and leafing through cookbooks looking for what I might bake on Saturday.

When I turned 12, Mother took me and my friend, Allison, into the den, handed us each four yards of fabric and a pattern for a jumper. It took a few tries before I got the hang of sewing, and I shed some tears of pure frustration as I cycled between throwing the dress into the trash can and reluctantly retrieving it again. I kept sewing up the neck of the jumper to which mother would patiently reply, "As you sew, so shall ye rip." (Actually, the no-neck jumper might not have been a bad invention. I could have hawked it as "The perfect solution for teenage bad-hair days, no worry about unsightly breakouts, ugly glasses. Just put on your no-neck jumper—handsewn with love by Becky.") In spite of my exasperation, Allison and I beamed with pride when we finally slipped on the dresses of our own making.

Knowing how we enjoyed the process of imagination and creation as children, why do we, as modern millennial parents, feel pressured to buy our children ready-made pleasure?

I looked out the door of the Dairy Queen and watched as my nephew enthusiastically turned the wheel-on-a-stick. In his mind, however, this wheely deal could have been an 18-wheeler or a fighter jet or a speed boat. Whatever it was, he looked like he was having a ball.

Perhaps some rocks, a stick, and a wheel is all we ever needed after all.

Look at the birds of the air; they do not sow or reap or store away...and yet your heavenly Father feeds them. Are you not much more valuable than they?

MATTHEW 6:26

Simplicity, simplicity, simplicity!
I say, let your affairs be as two or three,
and not a hundred or a thousand...keep your
account on your thumbnail.
—Henry David Thoreau

Growing up To Be a Child

I once wrote an entire book on the subject of staying childlike about life and God, called *Still Lickin' the Spoon*. During the process of writing, I came up with a little poetic ditty about the way I wanted to live the rest of my life with more child-like joy. (Someday I plan to do a whole album of these tunes and call it "Ditties from Becky: Songs to Embarrass Your Children By") You have to imagine singing it while doing a little soft-shoe shuffle. Louis Armstrong would be the vocalist I'd choose to perform this tune, if I were producing this cut. So try to sing it to yourself with a gravelly, all-the-time-in-the-world, *What a Wonderful World* kind of voice.

Growing Up to Be a Child

Mud-puddle miracles
Doodle-bug designs
Bursts of fun with bubblegum
Oh, to see life as a child!

"I love you's" big as rainbows
"I'm sorrys" from the heart

A kiss goodnight, a bear hug tight
To love as would a child!

"Let the children come to Me,"
He said with arms flung wide
Don't stop me now—
I'm comin', too
For I'm a child inside.

I want to laugh from the belly
Risk playing a clown—
I'm giving up on growing up

Think I'll just start growing d
                              o
                               w
                                n

Oh, yeeeaahhh.
(ta-dum-DUM)

12

Can Wee Talk?

Have you noticed, as I have, how careful parents are to use socially correct and psychologically healthy methods of speaking to their children these days? Parent/child communication has gone from "Come here" and "Stop that" to discourses only a psychoanalyst could love. Why does our generation of parents feel obligated to gently present a suggestion to our children? "Honey, when you finish that creative project you're working on, if you don't mind, I'd like you to begin thinking about starting some getting-ready-for-bedtime activities." Whatever happened to the simplicity of "Time for bed, kiddo"?

What's really hilarious is when our children begin to psycho-babble in our direction. Perfect example: I was shopping in a local drug store when across the Pain Relief aisle I happened to see a little boy, probably about age three, calmly sitting in the cart as his preoccupied mother cruised the Antacids.

Just then, I overheard the child ask with the empathy of a trained therapist, "Mother, are you happy?"

"Well, yes, Jonathan," she replied thoughtfully. "As a matter of fact, I am."

"Are you very, very happy?"

"Yes, Honey," she repeated patiently, "I'm very, very happy."

I couldn't help thinking, *I'm feeling some transactional analysis in the air. This kid's making sure "I'm okay, Mom's okay" before he lowers his self-centered boom on her.* I was right.

"That's very good, Mother," the child nodded approvingly, "because I need to tell you that I really need to get out of this store. Right now. I'm tired and I'm about to become upset with you."

Actually, I have to confess, I know all too well what it feels like to be on the receiving end of a pint-sized child psychologist's feedback.

One evening when the kids were small, after a late-bedtime fiasco on an evening with no help from a late-working, stressed-for-success daddy, I'd come to the end of my patience. I ordered the boys to bed, plunked Rachel on the couch, and sentenced her to lie there until I could get a grip on myself. I began furiously loading the dishes into the dishwasher, grumbling to myself all the while until, like a balloon out of air, I exhausted my anger. Rachel, noticing a quieting in the kitchen, bravely peeked over the back of the couch. She smiled knowingly and spoke in a maternal tone.

"Mother, are you ready to behave now?"

My good friend Gracie Malone and I were laughing about the way some children behave like miniature adults, when she suddenly remembered an incident with one of her grandkids. The whole Malone clan had dined together at a local Mexican restaurant. After a long and satisfying meal, her young grandson raised his small hand and motioned the waiter over to the table with the aplomb of a small celebrity. "Waiter," he said, as everyone sat opened mouthed around the table, "the enchiladas were *excellent*."

Occasionally my mother will pass on a precocious-grandchild story from some sweet mutual friends of ours, Taylor and Shalmir Nichols. The most recent report was a perfect illustration of the psycho-savvy of the current knee-cap-high generation. Seems Shalmir's three-year-old granddaughter, Abby, recently entered the world of preschool. A little boy in her class had apparently been giving Abby a hard time. "He even pushed me today," Abby cried to her mother, her tiny arms outstretched in exasperation.

"Oh, my!" her mother empathized. "What did you tell him?"

Abby put hands to hips and in no uncertain terms explained, "I told him to 'Stop the Violence!' "

I love it. But before long, I fear, preschoolers will be coloring "harassment suits" and filing "wrongful pushing" complaints in Wee Little Law School Learning Centers across the nation.

In spite of the infiltration of self-help language and lawyer talk into the Kindergarten ranks, there also remains a sweetness and innocence to childrens' conversations that can, without warning, zap the logic right out of an average, upstanding grown-up.

Taylor plays "Bampaw" to Shalmir's "Gramma." He's a Santa Claus look-alike (without the beard), a lawyer by profession, and tender-hearted by personality.

One evening, as our family visited around my parents' kitchen table, Taylor shared the following. "I took my grandson, little J.T., to the park on a beautiful afternoon. He was having such a good time, but at one point he paused from his running and swinging and sliding, ran over, and propped both elbows on my knees. Then he looked up at me with dreamy eyes and asked, 'Bampaw, could we stay here forever?'"

"What did you tell him?" I asked Taylor. With the wisdom of the ages, Counselor Taylor replied, "If you want to, J.T."

Sometimes our best efforts at parenting by the book are blown apart by one big-eyed child tugging at the sleeve of our heart.

Now, analyze THAT.

When I was a child, I talked like a child, I thought like a child, I reasoned like a child.

1 CORINTHIANS 13:11

What children expect from grown-ups is not to be "understood," but only to be loved, even though this love may be expressed clumsily or in sternness.
—**Carl Zucker**

Pint-sized Psychology

No matter how hard you try, you can't baptize cats.

When your mom is mad at your dad, don't let her brush your hair.

If your sister hits you, don't hit her back. They always catch the second person.

Never ask your 3-year-old brother to hold a tomato.

You can't trust dogs to watch your food.

A pencil without an eraser may as well just be a pen.

Never hold a dustbuster and a cat at the same time.

Part III

Home for Bewildered Mothers

13

Wanted: Crazy Mothers

The year was 1950. A young boy wanted to make a Super-8 movie for a Boy Scout project. His mother was not the type who says, "Go outside and play; I don't want that stuff in the house." She gave him free rein of the house, letting him convert it into his film studio, moving furniture, putting backdrops over things. She bought him 30 cans of cherries and dumped them into a pressure cooker when he needed an oozy red goop. She helped him make costumes and even acted in his films. The son's name? Steven Spielberg.

"In creative families," wrote the authors of *The Creative Spirit,* "there is a different feeling in the air; there's more breathing space."

There's something I admire about good-hearted crazy mothers like Mrs. Spielberg, women who rhumba to the beat of a different drum-ba and allow their youngsters to dance freely around them (within safe boundaries, of course). In fact one of my favorite posters is of a woolly sheep dyed bright purple. The caption underneath says, "I was normal once. I didn't like it." Most of us can fondly recall a teacher or a mom in our neighborhood whose very presence allowed us space to breath, to create, to play. Wouldn't it be great, at least occasionally, to be that kind of woman for our own children and their friends?

Another Mom Spielberg-like character recently emerged on the silver screen in the charming movie, *Hope Floats*. Though there were seemingly more important characters and themes, the actress who stole *my* heart was the off-beat matriarch of the small Texas home, played by Gena Rowland. Had I seen this movie when I was in my mid-twenties, I might have adopted her as the poster model for right-brained mothers.

This peculiar grandmother made her livelihood (and it *was* lively) sewing up dozens of stuffed animals and displaying them—inside the house and on the front lawn—in creative array. Not stuffed as in toy animals, but stuffed as in taxidermied critters. (Her specialty was bunny purses—with real rabbit heads. She never killed them, they come to her dead and in her own words, "I bring them to life.")

But what I enjoyed most about this unique character was her no-nonsense approach to nonsense. When her young grandson, Travis, appeared in his green turtle suit one morning, without comment this accommodating grandmother served the afternoon soup in turtle shells. She was obviously game for whatever Travis felt like being on any given day. If he was in a circus-y mood, he was outfitted with a clown face and brightly colored suit. If he was in the mood to be a puppy, Grandma was happy to sew him a pair of black felt ears and pet "Fido" as he walked about on all fours. All this without fanfare. It was simply a fact of life that in Grandma's house, imagination was not just a welcome guest, it was a permanent resident.

"Remind you of someone?" my friend and next-door neighbor, Melissa, whispered as we sat in the theater observing these scenes. I laughed. Everyone in our neighborhood knew our lastborn son, Gabe, almost never appeared out of costume during his early childhood years. He was always caped or masked or, at the very least, propped. Gabe's costumes were his identity: preschool power clothes. After all, without them someone might mistake him for a mild-mannered, average Clark Kent kid, rather than the incredible wowie zowie superhero he really was.

I got some strange looks as, flanked by a three-foot Dick Tracy in a banana yellow fedora and matching trenchcoat, I took my seat in the pew each Sunday. (He was Detective Tracy for a good six months.) People couldn't help but stare as I wheeled a miniature replica of a fireman in red slicker, hat, and "gas mask" (a bright orange pollen mask) up and down grocery store aisles. He was such a happy kid, and I was such a tired mother, that I preferred to let his imaginative playwear out of the closet, rather than argue with him over preschool convention. Though I know my indulgence with Gabe often embarrassed an older brother or sister, they each, in their own way, came to appreciate their mother for the irregular person she was—and is. Though I'm lacking many Good Mother attributes, one trait makes me very proud of myself: I've never been accused of being overly sensible.

In fact, I'll never forget the afternoon I went to pick up my oldest boys, Zeke and Zach, from a visit with a friend. They must have been about six and seven years old.

"Mom," Zach complained as soon as he plopped himself in the front seat of the car, "it was raining outside. There were great mud puddles everywhere, and Jason's mother wouldn't even let us play in them." Big pause, big sigh, and then he added, "I'm so glad you aren't sensible like all the other kids' moms." Little Zeekle (as Zach called him back then) furiously nodded his head up and down in rapt agreement.

A few years after the mud puddle incident, I came across a delightful essay called "My Mother Barked Like a Seal," by Jeanmarie Coogan, who wrote of her own quirky mother. She explained how this dramatic woman, full of mischief and fun, would alternately entertain and embarrass Jean-marie as a child. But there came a day when Jeanmarie real-ized she had it pretty good after all, as far as mothers go. She recalled her mom passing by a tree where a "bunch of us were dizzily swaying in the top branches." Rather than shrieking with fear, Jeanmarie's mother said, "I didn't know you could climb so high." Then she added, "That's terrific! Don't fall!" As her mother walked away, one boy, writes Coogan, "spoke for us all."

" 'Wow,' " he said softly, " 'Wow.' "

Similarly, the movie *Hope Floats* showcased a grown daughter (played by Sandra Bullock) who grew up with some ambivalence over her unconventional mother. But this same mother who sometimes embarrassed her also pos-sessed an upbeat and creative mind, capable of visualizing better things ahead for her daughter and granddaughter— both of whom had suffered a tremendous emotional blow when the husband/daddy walked out on them. It would be this crazy mother who would help her adult daughter appre-ciate the precious moments whizzing by before it was too late to capture them. ("It's the worst kind of extravagance," she told her daughter in exasperation, "the way you are wasting your chances.") Though Rowland's character had some emotional growing to do of her own—particularly in showing sensitivity to her daughter's deep pain—she ulti-mately exemplified courage, lovingly cocooned in humor.

There's something about slightly off-beat older women, with hearts of gold, that I blatantly admire. My own mother was a prime example, as are most of the women swinging from our family tree. When my kids were little, they were watching a re-run of "I Love Lucy," when they all turned their heads in unison toward me and asked, "Mom, is that GRANNY?" Having lived—and laughed—with my mother for many years, I can easily see how they drew this conclusion.

I've noticed that "characters"—original women, unafraid of outlandish fun—tend to raise resilient and creative off-spring. If they have family dysfunctions, at least they have the decency to make them seem entertaining. And I always say, "Better to fail with a bit of flair and drama than to fail quietly and miserably in anonymity."

I'm thankful for the women I come from—all of them smart cookies, sprinkled with just the right amount of mixed nuts. I hope to continue to float in their footsteps—and rhumba to the beat of a different drum-ba.

Some of our women amazed us.

LUKE 24:22

I once complained to my father that I didn't seem to be able to do things the same way other people did. Dad's advice? "Margo, don't be a sheep. People hate sheep. They eat sheep."

—**Margo Kaufman**

Signs of Advanced Motherhood

Maybe it starts when you realize rock concerts give you a headache. Or that you're offering to cut up other people's food. Or you catch yourself ending a discussion with, "Because I'm the Mother, that's why!"

You've reached a new level of motherhood. All the warning signs are there. You know you've crossed the threshold into advanced "Mommydom" when...

You count the sprinkles on each kid's cupcake to make sure they're equal.

You want to take out a contract on the kid who broke your son's favorite toy car and made him cry.

You have time to shave only one leg.

You hide in the bathroom to be alone.

Your child throws up and you catch it.

Someone else's kid throws up at a party and you keep eating.

You've mastered the art of placing large quantities of pancakes and eggs on a plate without anything touching.

Your child insists that you read *Once Upon A Potty* out loud in the lobby of Grand Central Terminal, and you do it!

You hope ketchup is a vegetable because it's the only one your child eats.

You fast-forward through the scene when the hunter shoots Bambi's mother.

You obsess when your child clings to you upon parting during his first month at school, then obsess when he skips in without looking back the second time.

You can't bear to give away baby clothes … it's so final.

You hear your mother's voice coming out of your mouth when you say, "NOT in your good clothes!"

You stop criticizing the way your mother raised you.

You read that the average five-year-old asks 437 questions a day and feel proud that your kid is "above average."

You hire a sitter because you haven't been out with your husband in ages, then spend half the night checking on the kids.

You say at least once a day, "I'm not cut out for this job," but you know you wouldn't trade it for anything!

14

It Takes a Village
to Help a Becky

A few years ago, we moved our family into a rickety old 865-square-foot cabin to be close to nature and to, uh-hum, *simplify* our lives. Gabe was three years old at the time. The first night in the cabin was a genuinely rustic experience—no phone, no water, no electricity. There were no frills or thrills on our countryside hills. Gabe woke up the next morning after a fitful night's sleep, walked to the closet, and put on his coat. He waved a fond farewell as he announced, "I'm goin' home now." It was easy to tell he was thinking, *This has been interesting, but let's get back to reality, gang.*

"But, Sweetheart," I carefully explained, dropping to one knee so I could meet him eye to eye, "this *is* our new home. It's where we're going to live from now own."

He looked at me as though I'd just grown a tulip out of one nostril.

"But this house is BROKEN!" he wailed.

Soon after we bought our cabin, Scott took the money we'd saved and built a nice shell of a home around us. It was a lovely two-story Victorian house—at least to passersby. But in reality it was like a Hollywood stage set. When you walked through the door, past the outside walls, you took a little inner maze-like path to the 865-square-foot cabin where we actually lived.

Over the years, as we could afford it, Scott would knock out walls and build on a room until finally, ten years later, our home is almost finished. He built the second story two years ago, with one minor detail missing. He refused to build stairs to the second story. We have three choices when it comes to ascending and descending to and from the second story. First, there's the leaning ladder. Secondly, there's the rope, which tends to be the descending method of choice. My kids literally come swinging down to breakfast on a rope, like Tarzan.

Finally, there's the rock climbing wall. The rock climbing wall is the reason Scott refused to build stairs. "We'll need that extra space for our ropes and belays," he reasoned with all the logic of a mental patient. And so, our family is literally climbing the walls.

Sometimes this worries me. After all, how long will our children have to spend in therapy to undo this crazy environment in which we are raising them? Add to this the fact that Martha Stewart not only doesn't live here, she'd probably rather do without pinking shears than drop by for a visit. *Good Housekeeping* is a magazine I never buy, simply out of respect for its publishers. It would not be fair to place a magazine with such a self-described title on a coffee table littered with a teenager's sunflower seed hulls and a child's day old grilled cheese sandwich.

One day, however, I received a note that lifted my sagging housekeeping spirits. It was from a friend of Zeke's, one of the many teenagers who often stopped by the wildlife habitat that we so lovingly call "home." It read, "Dear Becky, I just want to thank you for having me over. I love coming to your house…" I smiled with pleasure, then read the next phrase, chuckling aloud, "…because there's nothing we can do to mess it up."

One thing I've come to realize about my less than perfect housekeeping is that a little love and laughter and flexibility in a home will cover a multitude of dirty dishes and frozen pizzas.

Besides, it also gave me the opportunity to think creatively about how to solve my order-impairment.

"Let's face the facts, Becky," I said to myself one day. "You've given homemaking a good 15-year try. You always have the best intentions when you start to clean the house, but inevitably get waylaid cleaning out a drawer of baby pictures and then end up jotting down 'cute baby memories' on the remains of slightly used napkins. Maybe God's trying to tell you something."

As it turns out, He was. Though it took some trial and lots of error, I'm writing my way toward a clean and organized house. I think I've hit on a great deal here. A win-win for all concerned. I write a chapter, and it produces enough income to hire a dear lady to come clean once a week for a month. I write a column and I can pay a teenager, Courtney, to wash and fold clothes for two months! After ten years of writing and speaking, I'm finally even earning enough to pay Rose, another good friend, to be my part-time office assistant. Yet another crafty friend is helping me arrange furniture, drape old curtainless windows, and place pictures on walls in some orderly fashion. (She asked, with all kindness, if I'd allowed small children to hang them.)

Last Thursday, it just so happened that all four of my women/friend/helpers came over to do their jobs at one time. We had so much fun together that it reminded me of how it must have been in the Little House on the Prairie days of quilting and barn raisings. Where women banded together to accomplish a project, and work suddenly seemed more like play.

At one point I caught Rose laughing and shaking her head over my feeble and pitiful attempts at organizing. There were several boxes filled to the brim with items totally unrelated to each other—hand soap, book contract, earrings, stapler, a half-burned candle, a couple of checks to deposit—all of it loudly declaring that a creative person had made a hit-and-run effort. I shrugged my shoulders and weakly confessed, "What can I say? It takes a village to raise an idiot."

Many rewards came from that day when I admitted I was a failure at housekeeping and asked God to help me find a creative way to cope. Not only do I get to do what I love— which is write, minister to women, and spend time with my family, but the women who are helping me seem equally delighted. Each is fulfilling her God-given gift by working part-time in her area of expertise.

One day I found my teenage helper, Courtney, taping up little computer-generated signs around the house. On the dishwasher went, "We rinse our dishes before putting them in here, for a sparkling clean wash the first time!" In the laundry room there were nicely worded signs directing us as to what color of clothes to put where. When I complimented Courtney on her ability to organize, she looked at me and, with all sincerity, said, "Becky, y'all just make me feel so needed." The friend who is helping me with curtains and picture placement called last week and said, "Becky, you have no idea how much fun this has been for me. It's been just the diversion I needed during a tough time."

Then I realized what a great picture this Little Women scene in my crazy, cozy house really is. It's the way the Body of Christ could and should function—if we allow it to happen. We all have flaws and areas where God has left out a particular gifting. It's like we have these little pieces cut out of us, by design, like the indentations in puzzle pieces. Why? Perhaps besides being for our own humbling, they're God's way of making other people feel needed. Where you have a lacking, a brother or sister in Christ may have just the skill you need. If we will stop judging each other and simply connect and appreciate the Christian "village" around us, our work in this world will begin to feel a lot more like play.

For mothers who can't work at home or at a part-time job, I recommend getting help the old-fashioned way. Trade skills. You like to bake? Make a scrumptious cake for that gourmet-impaired friend, and perhaps she might love sorting through that closet you can't bring yourself to face. Or have a progressive housecleaning, or Christmas gift wrapping, or room painting party. Take one day and gather other mom friends to tackle chores for each other that are simply no fun to do alone.

All it takes is a humble spirit, a desperate need, and a few phone calls to other moms who are trying to fit life's puzzle pieces together as well. With a little planning and putting together of heads, a tiny village of women, intent on helping one another, might even give ol' Martha Stewart a jaunty run for her knick-knacks.

Two are better than one, because they have a good return for their work: If one falls down, his friend can help him up.

ECCLESIASTES 4:9,10

Why does life seek to organize with other life? When living beings link together they form systems that create more possibilities, more freedom for individuals. This is why life organizes, why life seeks systems, so that more may flourish.

—**Margaret J. Wheatley and Myron Kellner-Rogers**

Attention Children:
The Bathroom Door Is Closed!

Please do not stand here and talk, whine, or ask questions. Wait until I get out.

Yes, it is locked. I want it that way. It is not broken, I am not trapped.

I know I have left it unlocked, and even open at times, since you were born, because I was afraid some horrible tragedy might occur while I was in there but it's been years and I want some PRIVACY.

Do not ask me how long I will be. I will come out when I am done.

Do not bring the phone to the bathroom door.

Do not go running back to the phone yelling "She's in the BATHROOM!"

Do not begin to fight as soon as I go in.

Do not stick your little fingers under the door and wiggle them. This was only funny when you were two.

Do not slide pennies, Legos, or notes under the door. Even when you were two, this got a little tiresome.

If you have followed me down the hall talking, and are still talking as you face this closed door, please turn around, walk away and wait for me in a another room. I will be glad to listen to you when I am done.

Oh...

And yes, I still love you.

Mom

15

Nursing Home, Here I Come

Each child, as it comes through the birth canal, I'm convinced, takes a hearty scoop of its mother's brain cells. And I'm further convinced that at each of their birthdays, God dips out more of our brain cells and silently, invisibly donates them to our children. (Side note: my computer's spell check just suggested that my "brain cells" should be spelled "barnacles." Trust me, things are mentally deteriorating when your *word processor* starts making fun of you.) This is why, at the end of our lives, we're babbling and drooling in nursing homes, while our executive, well-educated children stop by to rub lotion on our hands and make sure our socks match. God gave them our brains, one subtle scoop at a time.

Or at least this is what I use for an excuse when my children are waiting alone on the curb at school, after some sport practice or field trip, realizing that—once again—their mother has forgotten to pick them up. It's truly a painful handicap, and the guilt I feel when I discover my error is enormous. The cell phone has certainly been a big help— if I remember to keep it turned on and the bill paid up, that is. Daughter Rachel sat me down about a month ago and gave me "the talk"—on my responsibilities as her parent.

"Mother," she said. "I know your forgetfulness is sometimes funny when you write about it, but it is NOT funny to me when I'm orphaned at school. It really bothers me and Gabe, so I'm asking you to do anything it takes. Write the reminder on your forehead, hire a plane to drop messages—just please, please, please try not to forget to pick us up anymore."

I hugged her and told her I was sorry that my senility seemed to have started so early, but that I would really, truly, try much, much harder to remember which kid I'm supposed to pick up when and where. "Forgive me?"

"Okay, but let's see some changes around here. Mom, I believe you can do it."

I nodded in the affirmative, feeling vaguely uneasy that the role reversal was on a nonstoppable roll.

The following week, I was at the school to pick up Gabe from football practice. Rachel, who had planned to stay late for Student Council meeting, saw me in the parking lot.

"Hey, Mom!" she shouted. I waved back and stuck my head out the window of the van. "Hey, there, Rach!" She jogged over to me and said, "I've decided to go ahead and go home with you now. I'm not feeling well. Let me just run to my locker and get my stuff—I'll be right back."

"Okay, I'll wait here," I said as she ran back into the school building to retrieve her things. Just then Gabe walked over to the van, threw his football gear into the back seat, and hopped in the front seat. Then I asked how his day went, started the van, and drove off.

After about a mile's worth of absentmindedly driving toward home, I realized, with a sickening thud, that I'd done it AGAIN. Whipping the van around, I drove as fast as I dared back toward the school. I hoped beyond hope that I could somehow make it back to the parking lot before my daughter felt like one of those poor, post-Rapture characters in *Left Behind*.

Just then the cell phone rang.

"MOM??" Rachel was incredulous. "WHERE ARE YOU?"

"I'm so sorry, Honey. I'm heading back your way."

"You FORGOT me? Less than ten seconds after I asked for a ride, you forgot me and just drove away? Do you realize how foolish I felt walking around and around the parking lot looking for our van. I thought I was crazy when I couldn't find it."

"See there's already a little silver lining there. You aren't crazy. It's still me! Rachey, it has nothing to do with my love for you. I love you more than anything and I'd never do this on purpose. It's just I'm operating on so few brain cells and the two or three I have in working order were used up greeting Gabe and starting the car. They just couldn't handle their job of remembering to wait for you, too."

"Mom," she said, her voice quivering with frustration, "if this goes in one of your books, I'm not going to laugh."

That was two weeks ago. Last night, I asked Rachel if she could remember any humorous episodes between her and me of late. "Why?" she asked.

"Because I'm writing a book on being a mother—to help other mothers feel better about themselves. Sort of give them material so they can say to themselves, 'At least I haven't gotten as bad as that wacky ol' Becky Freeman.'"

"Did you write about forgetting me in the parking lot the other day?"

"Not yet. You said if I did that you wouldn't laugh."

"Go ahead and write about it," she said. "I'm starting to think it's maybe…just a little bit…funny."

"That's my girl," I said with pride. "You're going to survive me yet."

"Yeah, but when you're old and in the nursing home, I'll get my revenge. I'm going to put your dress on backwards and mismatch your socks."

She lifted one eyebrow, doing her best to look sinister. Then she stopped, looked at me a little more closely, and shook her head.

"What?" I asked.

"Never mind," she said, as she walked away. "You're hopeless."

I looked down at myself to see what was so funny and discovered, to my great amusement, that my "I Am My Kid's Mom" T-shirt (the kids gave it to me as a memory aid) was on backwards, and that I was sporting one pink and one red sock.

I laughed to myself, then called down the hall to her disappearing form, "Hey, Rach, would you mind rubbing some lotion on my hands?"

Can a mother forget the baby at her breast...? Though she may forget, I will not forget you! See, I have engraved you on the palms of my hands.

ISAIAH 49:15,16

They tell you that you'll lose your mind when you grow older. What they don't tell you is that you won't miss it very much.

—**Malcolm Cowley**

Everything You Wanted To Know About God, And Were Afraid To Ask an Eight-Year-Old

Written by Danny Dutton, age 8, from Chula Vista, California, for his third-grade homework assignment to "Explain God."

One of God's main jobs is making people. He makes them to replace the ones that die so there will be enough people to take care of things on earth.

He doesn't make grown-ups, just babies. I think because they are smaller and easier to make. That way, He doesn't have to take up His valuable time teaching them to talk and walk. He can just leave that to mothers and fathers.

God's second most important job is listening to prayers. An awful lot of this goes on, since some people, like preachers and things, pray at times besides bedtime.

God doesn't have time to listen to the radio or TV because of this.

God sees everything and hears everything and is everywhere which keeps Him pretty busy. So you shouldn't go wasting His time by going over your mom and dad's head asking for something they said you couldn't have.

Jesus is God's Son. He used to do all the hard work like walking on water and performing miracles and trying to teach the people who didn't want to learn about God. They finally got tired of Him preaching to them and they crucified Him.

And now He helps His Dad out by listening to prayers.

You can pray anytime you want and they are sure to hear you because they got it worked out so one of them is on duty all the time.

Don't skip church to do something you think will be more fun like going to the beach. This is wrong! And, besides, the sun doesn't come out at the beach until noon anyway.

If you don't believe in God, besides being an atheist, you will be very lonely, because your parents can't go everywhere with you, like to camp, but God can.

It is good to know He's around you when you're scared in the dark or when you can't swim very good and you get thrown into real deep water by big kids.

But you shouldn't just always think of what God can do for you. I figure God put me here and He can take me back anytime He pleases.

And that's why I believe in God.

16

Have Grin, Will Travel

I was doing one of my favorite things—laughing and lunching with five other women friends, who are also speakers and authors. One of the ladies, a piece of chocolate cheesecake poised on her fork, asked, "Becky, how do you manage to be a mom of four kids, write books, and do traveling and speaking?"

"Well," I admitted, "I can't do it all. Not without some help. And though I've limited my out-of-town engagements to twice a month in the spring and fall, Scott's a great Mr. Mom in my absence. He's always been more of a 'women do the kids and homemaking thing' type guy, but lately he's become so maternal it's a little spooky. The last time I got home from a two-day engagement, he said, 'Now, the colored clothes have been laundered, but the whites still need to be done. Don't forget to add the bleach. And there's a list of groceries we need taped up on the fridge. Now Gabe has a birthday party in an hour, which I'll take him to. But Rachel is up in her room, and to tell you the truth, I think she needs a little bit of attention. She acts like she enjoys being alone, but I've found a little daily chat really perks her right up.' I felt like I was talking alternately to Dr. Spock and Heloise. Seriously, though, I think it's been good for him and for the kids to have bonding time without me."

"Have you found ways to make packing and traveling easier?" another friend, who writes how-to books, quizzed.

"Yes, actually, I think I have. The nice thing about traveling out of town for presentations is that you only need one suit. Since I may speak in South Carolina one week, and Wautuga, Florida the next, the audience is none the wiser. For example, 1998 was the Year of the Pink Jacket. 1999 was classic black and white. I wear black heels, faux pearl earrings and a pearl necklace with everything. You know, I think it's more complicated to decide what to wear to McDonald's than it is to pack for a trip now.

"Oh, and another thing I do to make traveling easier," I added, feeling suddenly very travel agency, "is to keep my makeup case packed at all times. I just put on my makeup straight from my travel bag, whether I'm at home or in the air or in Montana."

"Great idea," they agreed, one of them jotting down my little suggestions on a napkin with numbers beside them. I continued feeling oh-so-savvy until I remembered a recent incident that sort of blew a hole in my Travel Tip Talk.

"Y'all, I have to confess something. I'm unbelievably messy, even on the road."

"No!" the girls answered in mock horror.

"For example, I just hate cleaning that makeup bag out. So before long, I've got lids off the toothpaste tubes and hair pins sticking out of uncovered lipsticks. Not to mention old gum wrappers and leaky fingernail polish. It can get really nasty.

"The other day I was going through the X-ray check point at the airport and something in my bag—probably the lethal smell of mixed beauty products—caused some concern for the security personnel. One man, who looked of princely, perhaps Arabian, descent, asked if he could check my bag. 'Okay,' I told him, 'but it's not a pretty sight.' He unzipped the bag, took one look inside and yelled, "Oh, YUCK!" Then he began clucking his tongue like a scolding mother, muttering something in Arabic mingled with a few more yuck, yuck, yucks for good measure. Not daring to stick his hand inside my lethal makeup kit to search for explosives, he simply zipped it back up, giving everyone around us an exaggerated look of disgust—like he just examined a body bag or something—and dismissed me with, 'Go on, Lady. Jou just go on.'"

We all enjoyed a good laugh, and then my friend Gracie jumped in with affirmation. "Traveling with Becky is just incredible. I once went on a speaking trip with her and I boarded her van with my neat little suitcase. I paused before getting in, because I simply couldn't help noticing the wide assortment of things littering the van floor. Everything from boxes of books to Gabe's football helmet, old clothes, leftover junk food, empty soft drink cans...I mean, a homeless person could happily live in that van for a very long time. Before too long, as we drove along, I found myself finishing up a canned Coke and just tossed it over my shoulder—devil-may-care—to the pile in the back. Never even made a 'clink' when it landed."

"Is it really that bad?" the others quizzed.

I smiled. "I'm afraid so. But, Gracie, remember when I discovered I'd only packed one sock?"

"Oh, that's right! I kid you not, Becky found a matching anklet in the back of the van in less than two minutes."

"There are advantages to sloth," I replied pertly. Then, thinking about it more I added, "My motto is 'Just play the melody' whenever possible. I'd rather put my energies into people and fun than cleaning."

Gracie admitted, "I'm nothing like Becky. Neatness is my preference, but there's something wildly liberating about hanging out with her now and then. You just stop caring about the details and enjoy the ride. With her, it all comes out in the wash somehow."

"But what would you do," my friend Jane asked, "if you forgot something really important at home?"

"Well, this fall I was under a lot of pressure. I was booked to speak every single weekend for six weeks in a row. Never again! Combine that schedule with book deadlines, my absentmindedness, and my oldest son going through a 'growing up' crisis—and I was doing great just to remember to put my pants on my legs instead of over my head. I was speaking on a Friday and Saturday night in Oklahoma. It wasn't until I'd finished speaking on Friday evening that I remembered I'd only packed one suit."

"What did you do??"

"Well, the nice thing about a little family trauma now and then is that things like forgetting your clothes don't really seem like a big deal."

"How do you find the strength to go and encourage other women when your heart is breaking over some problem at home?" another friend, and mother of two, asked.

"That is so hard, I'll be honest with you. All I can say is that God does it through me, around me, because of, and in spite of me. I will usually confess to the audience at some point that I'm hurting, and ask for their prayers. Some of the sweetest sources of comfort, during trying times, have come from landing in a pack of new momma friends who

surround me with love and prayer, even though I'm sup-
posedly 'the minister.' I often arrive thinking I'll be a blessing
to others, and the truth is, women in the audience lift up and
bless me. Then, too, God seems to outdo Himself in letting
me know He's watching over my family while I'm away."

I paused, took a sip of iced tea, then settled back to finish
the story.

"On this particular trip, as I drove by fields of golden
wheat, I remember praying, *Lord, I'm so worried about my
son right now. I could really use a sign from you to help me
relax.* And just then I passed a handmade sign, black letters
on white plywood, that read, GOD RULES. Nothing else. No
'Sponsored by First Baptist Church' or 'Jesus Loves You at
Howard's Hardware.' Just GOD RULES sticking up in the
middle of a cow pasture. God gave me an actual SIGN.
Nobody can tell me He doesn't have a sense of humor. I was
sure my guardian angel had just flown it in and plunked it
down, and was probably pickin' hay out of his halo on his
way back to heaven."

"Okay, back to the clothes thing," the gal making the Tip
List said, "What did you do?"

"Well, I asked the event planner if I could go to Wal-
Mart—the only store open—during the workshop sessions.
She said, 'Sure!' so I headed out to the Sun-dried Tomato—
and to my relief and joy, found a brown suede jacket
wadded up under the back seat."

"I'm tellin' ya," Gracie interjected, "she could clothe Bul-
garia with the castoffs in her vehicle."

I rolled my eyes at Gracie and went on. "So I climbed in
the van, turned the key, realized I'd left my lights on and that
my battery had died. Before long, a kind deacon had mercy
on me, insisting I take his car to Wal-Mart while he charged
up my battery. People can be so nice!"

"And naive," teased Gracie.

"All right," I lowered my eyes at Gracie and with the sternness of a school teacher scolded, "That will be enough out of you, Missy." Then turning my head toward the others, I continued. "Anyway, it was dark by this point, but the man directed me to his car, and I drove to Wal-Mart. Within minutes, I found a nice khaki skirt and a pretty embroidered shirt, in olive green, that looked just too cute with my wrinkled, wadded-up jacket. Proud of my purchase, I headed to the parking lot and that's when I realized I had no idea what kind of car I'd just driven to the store. I'd just hopped in the front seat with the deacon's keys, driven to Wal-Mart, and walked away from the car without looking back at what I'd been driving. I passed the next 30 minutes, trying the key in about fifteen car doors until I finally hit the jackpot."

"Did the ladies at the church think you were nuts when you told them what happened?"

"You know," I mused, "I think they did. But I seem to inspire this pitiful benevolence in people. It's the 'bless her heart' response. Like 'Bless her heart, we'd better help this little gal out. She may never find her way home if we don't.' In general, I've found I make people feel considerably better about themselves, not so much by my motivational talks, but just by letting them watch me mess up."

My friends looked puzzled, a mix of awe and concern crossing their faces. I smiled, because only I know how far I've come. Used to be, I'd be stressed out to the point of near breakdown imagining disaster striking my family without my being home to protect them. The thought of packing, getting on a plane (and crashing), hauling books, and remembering three or four speeches provoked a low-grade panic. Now, it all seemed relatively easy. Plane delays, lost luggage, forgetting my notes—I've survived it all to live and laugh another day. Struggling to put into words how relaxed I've become with my own inadequacies and God's abilities to cover for me, I said, "I think I just blew a stress fuse at one point."

"What?"

"I realized one day I could go crazy trying to do everything perfectly and in order, or I could just relax and *be* crazy and let life happen. I realized that all the things I worried would happen to my kids never did. And some things I neglected to worry about did happen. But my worrying, in either case, did absolutely no good."

Since I seemed to have an audience of listening ears, I plunged recklessly into deeper spiritual waters. "I love the phrase from Scripture, 'Let it be.' It was what Mary said after struggling to accept the little news bulletin that she would be Christ's mother. At one point she gave up arguing 'How could this be?' and accepted that God Rules. 'Let it be unto me,' she said, 'according to Thy word.' So when I start to get panicky, I say to myself, 'Let it be'—and just let life unfold. I begin to chill out emotionally, slowing down on the inside of my head, and become serene, almost curious, about what God will do next."

I drove home from lunch that afternoon grateful for the place I am at 40 years of age: an absolute mess. But that's *okay*. It's been said that one of the advantages to living in a small town is that if you don't know what you're doing, someone else does. In the same way, an advantage to being God's child is that when I don't know what I'm doing, He does and He often sends one of His kids or invisible angels to help me out. He's also just as near to my children. Though I want to be there for them always, at every point of felt pain, that can't happen. I'm comforted by something Amy Carmichael wrote in a letter to a friend far away from home, where all, apparently, was not well. "Don't forget when you imagine, all but see and hear and desperately feel, your loved one's pain, there is one thing that eludes you. That is the grace that is being given, the Presence that is there." When Zach and Zeke were little, one of their favorite books repeated the phrase, "God goes with you EVERY-WHERE!" That grace, that Presence, reaches not only to us as we travel, but also to where we wish we could be. Including hovering over and around our loved ones.

I pulled the van up next to my red barn-shaped mailbox, interrupting my deep thoughts with a shallow one. *I love mail.* I reached in and pulled out a stack of letters. One of them just happened to be from the deacon and his wife who'd been kind (and brave) enough to lend me their car in Oklahoma. Enclosed with the note was a credit card. The note read, "Dear Becky, We found this gas card in the floor of our vehicle and, for a few minutes, just couldn't imagine how it got there. Then we laughed as we thought, of course, it had to be you. Becky, you made our day with your inspiring talks and your scatterbrained personality."

What can I say? Somebody has to prove that God can really use anybody, anywhere, anytime for any purpose He needs to accomplish. Yes, even mothers who constantly mix up their own children's names, or can't remember why they've just walked into a room, or don't have a clue why their hairbrush is in the freezer.

Our life journey here is pretty short. We can eat each moment up with worry about our kids, our responsibilities—or fuming over delays and disappointments. Or we can do what we can and give God the rest. Save the time you've been worrying and take a nice nap instead, trusting in His hovering Presence.

"Let it be." All is well.

You'll travel safely, you'll neither tire nor trip. You'll take afternoon naps without a worry, you'll enjoy a good night's sleep. No need to panic over alarms or surprises, or predictions that doomsday's just around the corner, because God will be right there with you; He'll keep you safe and sound.

PROVERBS 3:23-26, THE MESSAGE

Will you give me yourself?
Will you come travel with me?
—Walt Whitman

Part IV

Teenagehood

(or "The Toddler Reprise")

17

Embarrass Your Children by Breathing

Anne Lamott is one of my favorite writers, an off-the-wall Christian whose work will probably never be published by a mainstream Christian publisher because of her gut-level, sometimes crude honesty. But I like this lady's work, very much, with all her insecurities and humor and grief and hope laid right out there in print, her heart on paper. In her hilarious and poignant diary of her son's first year of life, she wrote about her fears of becoming a mother:

"The worst thing, worse even than sitting around crying about that inevitable day when my son will leave for college, worse than thinking about whether or not in the meantime to get him those hideous baby shots he probably should have but that some babies die from, worse than the fears I have when I lie awake at 3:00 in the morning (that I won't be able to make enough money and will have to live in a tenement house where the rats will bite our heads while we sleep, or that I will lose my arms in a tragic accident and will have to go to court and diaper my son using only my mouth and feet and the judge won't think I've done a good enough job and will put Sam in a foster home), worse even than the fear I feel whenever a car full of teenagers drives past my house going 200 miles an hour on our sleepy little street, worse than thinking about my son being run over by one of those teenagers—worse than just about anything else is the agonizing issue of how on earth anyone can bring a child into this world knowing full well that he or she is eventually going to have to go through the seventh and eighth grades."

I think most of us would agree that surviving the seventh and eighth grade is the price to be paid for getting to go on with the rest of your life without ever being quite that totally insecure again. Simply walking through a junior high school cafeteria can be like tip-toeing through a landmine. Wearing the wrong shade of lipgloss or brand of jeans or tennis shoes, or—horrors!—the eruption of a pimple, can turn a "cool kid" into the unfortunate victim of this week's homeroom jokes.

Anne Lamott also wrote, "There is a beautiful poem by a man named Roy Fuller, which ends, 'Hurt beyond hurting, never to forget,' and whenever I remember those lines, which is often, I think of my father's death ten years ago this month, and I think about seventh and eighth grades."

Oh, my, do I identify. Judith Viorst wrote a poem in her wonderful collection, *If I Were in Charge of the World,* about the way a young heart can be so easily broken, ripped and torn like so much paper. How we wait during those long days for someone to come to our aid and patch up our heart with tape and glue and kindness. The poem concludes, "But until then—the pain, the pain, the pain!" I first read this poem, written for children, when I was in my thirties and taking an English Lit. class. I found myself crying when I came to the last line, filled with compassion for the lonely little outcast I once was during those in-between years—those no-man's-land, middle-age years between adorable childhood and driving a car.

I don't know how it happened, perhaps because God thought I'd endured enough during my own middle school years—but he spared me the agony of watching my children endure the same misfit label I miserably wore. In our small-town school of Lone Oak, Texas, Rachel and Gabe (the two kids left at home) are actually considered very cool. I'm grateful that the two of them seem to be aware of this great good fortune, and I've noticed they are kind to other kids, no matter their social "rank."

However, Rach and Gabe have come to realize that having me, a lifelong Nerd, as their *mother* can be more than a bit unsettling. It amazes me, actually, how little it takes for a middle-aged mother to embarrass or annoy her young teenagers. By the time they hit the mid-teens and the upper-high-school years, their blooming self-confidence gives them more tolerance for the presence of Mom, the Ultimate Nerd. But twelve- to fourteen-year-olds tend to stay pretty edgy around their mothers most of the time. They never know when Mom could explode—saying something unforgivably asinine in public.

Like, "Hi there."

Though my status as "a book writer" helps some, it doesn't take me off the Nerd hook. (As an aside, nobody calls me a hoity-toity "author" in Lone Oak; I'm a "book writer" and that's that.) Imagine Mel Gibson revealing that his real father is Austin Powers, or that his uncles are Dumb and Dumber, and you can capture the uneasy feelings my parental presence provokes in my more-suave offspring, especially at school events. It must be a little something of what Jimmy Carter felt whenever brother Billy showed up at the White House for tea.

Last week, for example, I went to a school ball game. When I heard the announcer say, "That was Mark Johnson doing a fine job on the tackle," I stood up and whooped and cheered.

"Sit down, Mother," my kids hissed.

Reluctantly, but obediently, I sat down, "But, y'all," I explained, "that was a great play, and if Mark didn't make the tackle, the other team would've made a touchdown."

Gabe slapped his forehead in exasperation, as if to say, "How many times am I going to have to endure this?"

"Mom," he carefully explained, as if he were talking to a nursery-school child, "Mark Johnson is on the other team!"

"Oh," I said.

Gabe nodded, relieved that none of his friends had seen my faux pas.

"But, Gabe," I added sincerely, "that was a great tackle."

At that, Gabe stood up and found another seat about a football-field length away from me.

Then there's the problem of parking. I usually drop off the kids at the stadium gate, then park my car. The oddest thing about football stadiums. Both halves of the field look exactly alike. Both sides have ticket takers, twin snack bars, and identical bathrooms. (I've also discovered that unless you really look carefully, the "Boys" and "Girls" bathrooms are nearly identical in appearance. I've unnerved a few un-zipped men with this mix-up more than once.) Inevitably, when I leave the stadium with the kids in tow and they ask the all-important question: "Mom, which side of the field did you park on?"—I'm stumped.

We wander around the parking lot like the children of Israel encircling Mount Sinai. I can hear Rachel and Gabe breathing evil threats against me under their breath, no matter how cheerful I try to be about "our car-searching adventure." Making little jokes like, "Where in the World is our Car, man—San Diego?" falls on humorless ears. It always turns out okay, so I don't really understand how our wandering in circles upsets them so. Eventually, everyone else finds their cars and we can easily see that the only car left in the parking lot must be ours.

Friday night, on our third lap around the parking lot, I spied a friend. For years, this kind man has volunteered to take the sport photos at our high school football games. His name—and I must admit I just love it—is Buster Klem. Buster always wears a baseball hat backwards and is the most perpetually cheerful fellow I've ever met. He loves to give me a good-natured teasin' about the time I fell down an entire flight of stairs during the ceremonial "When I Walk Through the Storm" at Rachel's eighth-grade graduation.

Anyway, as I spied my buddy Buster walking near the bleachers, I ran up to him and yelled, "Hey, Buster!" This, before Rachel and Gabe could advise me that the man I saw was not, after all, Buster Klem. He looked shocked, however, as if he'd been caught doing something he shouldn't be doing. (In the south, anyone caught doing wrong is often called down with a generic, "Hey, Buster." I have no idea why, so don't ask.)

When I was about a foot from Buster's look-alike face, I smiled weakly and said, "Oops. You know what? You aren't Buster." He just stared at me, careful to avoid any sudden movements. Then for good measure, I added, "But a friendly 'Hey!' to ya anyway." I kept on walking, not daring to look back at Rachel and Gabe, who were exchanging looks I was certain I didn't want to see.

These are just a small sampling of the typical, everyday Mom Humiliations visited upon my kids.

Every once in awhile, I really hit the Nerd jackpot. For some reason, several of my more impressive fiascoes of the past couple of years have occurred on football fields.

This past summer, Gabe went to a special football camp sponsored by Jay Novecek at a local college. On the last day, Gabe was to be in the camp play-offs. He called and asked that I come to watch, describing in minute detail his team's jerseys so I'd be seated on the right side of the field. I came and watched. He played a great game, and I never yelled for the wrong team. Not even once. Afterwards, I wanted to find Gabe and congratulate him, but he was nowhere to be found.

Finally, I picked up my lawn chair, and heaving a back-pack of canned soft drinks onto my shoulder, trudged across an open field to look for him near the athletic building. When I paused mid-field to look around once more for some sign of Gabe, I saw a mass of white helmets on top of large football-player bodies running, like a herd of moose, towards me.

I had no choice but to make a dash, backpack and lawn-chair in tow, toward the goal line. It was that or stand and get tackled by giant linemen, for I'd just unwittingly walked on the field in the middle of a high school scrimmage game that had begun right after Gabe's game on the same field. I ran as fast as my little legs could carry me, cellulite jiggling in all the wrong places. I couldn't help but overhear comments coming from the sidelines. "Who is that lady?" "WHAT'S she carrying?" "Somebody get that kook off the field!" Once over the goal line, I just shook out my chair and sat down for a victory drink.

Needless to say, when I finally found Gabe, he thanked God several times for sparing him from seeing the first-ever Mom and Lawnchair touchdown run.

After I'd breathlessly shared my play-by-play football debut with Gabe, I laughed and casually reached out to give him a hug. But he pulled away, shooing my outstretched arms as if they were two bothersome weasels. Though it hurt my feelings, I gave him his space to grunt and saunter around the other football players. Once in the van, however, I asked him, "Gabe, why didn't you let me hug you?"

"Because I'm getting too old for that."

"But, Gabe, the other night when you had a migraine, you asked me to stay with you and rub your back until you fell asleep."

"Well, it's okay for you to touch me when I'm in pain—at home. Don't ever do it in public though, even if my head is about to explode."

"Then can I hug you at home?"

"Yes, but not too often."

I think I've finally got the No-Touching Rules down. I can hug Gabe at home, every third day, unless it's raining or there's a full moon. A one-arm-around-the-shoulder hug is preferred over a full bodied embrace. However, if said child is in pain, a full bodied bear hug—accompanied by a backrub—is permissible. If, that is, there's no one at home but the family, and I check to make sure we aren't too close to a window where a neighbor could see.

It's really hard, sometimes, having such cool kids.

Still, with all its ups and downs and near-misses, I love having these self-conscious, fragile human beings around the house. Especially every third day when it's not raining and the moon is full.

Listen to your father, who gave you life, and do not despise your mother when she is old.

PROVERBS 23:22

When I was a boy of fourteen, my father was so ignorant that I could hardly stand to have the old man around. But when I got to be twenty-one, I was astonished at how much the old man had learned in seven years.
—**Mark Twain**

Thoughts on Raising Children

by Robert Fulghum
from It Was on Fire When I Lay Down on It

1. Children are not pets.

2. The life they actually live and the life you perceive them to be living is not the same life.

3. Don't take what your children do too personally.

4. Don't keep scorecards on them—a short memory is useful.

5. Dirt and mess are a breeding ground for well-being.

6. Stay out of their rooms after puberty.

7. Stay out of their friendships and love-life unless invited in.

8. Don't worry that they never listen to you; worry that they are watching you.

9. Learn from them; they have much to teach you.

10. Love them long; let them go early.

Finally, a footnote. You will never really know what kind of parent you were or if you did it right or wrong. Never. And you will worry about this and them as long as you live. But when your children have children and you watch them do what they do, you will have part of an answer.

18

Back Talk, for Your Listening Entertainment

When I first began writing about my children—the cute, the bad, and the funny—it never occurred to me that one day the storytelling tables might turn. Never thought that my toddlers, with adorable antics aplenty, might grow up to be keen-witted teens with comebacks aplenty. Like all mothers, I'm faced with the problem of how to handle a teen's occasional sarcasm—or, as we say in the south, "back talk." The compounded dilemma for me, as a humorist, is that their smart replies are often really funny. I find myself losing all objectivity as their mother, and rushing instead for my pen and paper to take notes on their comedic comebacks.

A prime example of too-funny-not-to-laugh dialogue occurred a few weeks ago, when Scott and I, along with Rachel and Gabe, boarded a plane for Colorado. I'd hoped this Colorado vacation would be a special bonding time for the four of us, now that the two oldest boys, Zach and Zeke, were out of the nest. I smiled over at Scott and twelve-year-old Gabe (bonding team one) buckling into their plane seats, as fifteen-year-old Rachel and I (bonding team two) took the two seats opposite our menfolk. It felt oh so Father Knows Best-y, so Mr. and Mrs. Cleaver-ish. I gave a little wave to Ward and the Beav before settling into my airline seat. Suddenly, a sharp pain in the lower right side of my abdomen broke my happy family bonding fest.

"Rachel," I said quietly, my voice weakening. "Don't be alarmed, but I think I've got either a tumor or appendicitis or a bad case of gas." I searched my daughter's face for some shred of sympathy. With all the sinister tenderness of Nurse Ratched of *One Flew Over the Cuckoo's Nest*, she gripped my forearm and said solemnly, "Mother, it better not be gas."

"Terrific!" I shot back, suddenly gaining strength. "So while your poor mother is suffering in agony, your first impulse is to pray, "Dear Lord, let it be a tumor! Or at the very least, appendicitis." In spite of my pain, I had to admit I was getting pretty tickled at the dialogue sparking between us. Between clenched teeth, I managed to quip, "Oh, great, now I think I have laughing gas!"

"Mom, shhhh! You're disturbing the passengers."

"Oh, well," I whispered as loudly as I dared, "far be it from me to upset the happy passengers with my little TUMOR flare-up."

"Mom," she replied with a tone of finality, imitating Arnold Schwartzeneger from the movie, *Kindergarten Cop*, "It's NOT a tu-MAH!"

Once we landed in the beautiful Rockies, I began to feel much better. So rather than checking into Denver's nearest emergency room, the four of us hopped a rental car and headed toward our mountain getaway. As we drove along under a wide open sky of pure blue, I looked over at Scott. So handsome, even after twenty-three years of marriage. Awash with sentimentality, I recalled our early days as husband and wife. Since we married as teenagers, we'd shared so many "firsts" together.

"Gabe and Rach," I said, glancing toward the back seat. "I was just thinking about how many things your father has taught me over the years. Like how to snow ski."

"Only took four hours to get her skis on and get her vertical," Scott added, thoughtfully.

"And," I looked tenderly at my husband, choosing to ignore his comment, "you taught me how to ice skate and water ski and canoe through white water rapids."

"Becky," Scott glanced my way for a split second before looking out the windshield again, "you cried all the way down the Guadelupe River. You said you'd divorce me if I ever put your toes near white water again. Said you'd wrap a kayak around my ..."

"Now, Honey," I replied, "let's be nice. The point wasn't that I ENJOYED learning any of the things you taught me. The point was you taught me to do them. Remember—you even taught me how to drive!"

"What?!?" the kids shouted in unison from the back.

"Yes," I nodded, explaining. "I'd only had my driver's license about two months before I married your daddy and I'd never driven a stick shift. It was all we had, so he taught me how to drive our standard shift Opal hatchback."

"I'll never forget it either," Scott chimed in. "Drifting backwards down that hill, the whiplashing motion of our heads as you shifted gears and repeatedly stomped the brakes, the mile-long line of honking cars behind us ..."

"Dad?" Rachel asked, interrupting his description.

"Yes," came his absentminded reply. I could tell he was mentally trying to pull away from The Day My Wife Stopped Traffic.

"You really taught Mom how to ski and drive and stuff?"

"Yes, I guess I did."

"Well, Dad, do you know what that says about you?"

"What, Sweetie?"

"You don't have the gift of teaching."

Even though her remark was, in actuality, a double insult, the humor was just too fine for the Funny Girl in me to overlook. I suppose, in our family, with few exceptions, there's nothing we enjoy more than a good laugh at ourselves. At least we put the FUN in our dysFUNctions.

I was sharing this incident with a friend of mine, a single mother, who'd recently had to downsize their family home due to finances (and the lack thereof). Moving from a three-bedroom brick to a two-bedroom mobile home in a less-than-nice neighborhood was taking its toll on her teenage daughter's pride. One afternoon, my friend told her daughter, "You know, I think we need a better lock on that front door."

"Mother," her daughter replied, sarcasm seeping from every pore, "like a burglar is going to be stopped by a lock, when he could just huff and puff and blow the house *down*?"

In spite of the sassiness of the child's reply, we had to admit—it was a classic line.

Sure, there's a fine line between insulting each other and poking good-natured fun in a family. Sometimes the parent (especially the parent who loves to laugh) has to monitor that line, being sensitive to when a joke oversteps good-hearted humor and ends up hurting feelings. We discover, by trial and error, how best to express love and humor. Even with its inherent risks, I believe a family grows closer, and the teen years are more survivable, if we regularly enjoy a good laugh at ourselves.

Even wise King Solomon talked about the healing benefits of merriment. I should know—it cured my pesky tumor/appendicitis attack right up.

A cheerful heart is good medicine.

PROVERBS 17:22

My mother had a great deal of trouble with me, but I think she enjoyed it.
—**Mark Twain**

Important Things I've Learned from Kids

1. If you're gonna draw on the wall, do it behind the couch.

2. Ask "Why?" until you understand.

3. Even if you've been fishing for three hours and haven't gotten anything except poison ivy and a sunburn, you're still better off than the worm.

4. It doesn't matter who started it.

5. Ask for sprinkles.

6. If the horse you're drawing looks more like a dog, make it a dog.

7. If you want a kitten, start out asking for a horse.

8. Just keep banging until someone opens the door.

19

Sports Nut

Last night I sat high on the bleachers during a high school ball game, in pouring rain, huddled next to my friend Rose. Rain dripped from our lashes and noses, our hair looked like used carpet mats. Between chatting about our kids and this book, and watching the Buffaloes play football in mud up to their shins, something came from somewhere above my head and landed, with a heavy thud, in my lap.

"Oh, my goodness," Rose said, laughing incredulously. "What's that in your lap?"

"Rose," I said, my eyes wrinkled in stunned curiosity. "It looks like a huge wedge of pizza. Extra thick crust."

Rose just sat kind of blinking in confusion, and finally I mused aloud, "You know, this is a first for me. I got quite a shiner on my forehead last year from a cheerleader slinging hard candy. But I've never been pelted by a pizza."

I tossed the pizza between the bleachers to the ground below, and began to pick pepperoni out of my hair. *What we mother's won't endure for our kids,* I thought, as I sat soaking in rain, smelling of mozzarella and tomato sauce.

Through wind and rain and black-of-night games, we moms trudge ever forward toward the hard, cold bleachers—holding Styrofoam cups of bad lukewarm coffee in one hand, old quilts in the other—braving the elements (and now, flying pizza) for two universal purposes. We want to be there to cheer, should our child score a point; and we want to be ready should they need our medical insurance card and a ride to the emergency room.

Sometimes I think this whole "parents & kids & sports" thing is insane. There's danger involved on the field for our kids and in the stands for us parents. But as long as our children choose to live in the center of life's arena, rather than watch from the sidelines, their choices will always carry some risk, along with the glory. We parents get to experience, vicariously, their agonies and ecstasies. I'll never forget Zeke's high school football years. Particularly vivid are the agonies…

It was Friday football on a beautiful October evening in Texas. The crisp air, the band playing something patriotic and snappy, the Buffaloes' red uniforms, contrasted with the blue of the other team's, looked so lovely against the green field. (We women notice these things.)

All was bright and beautiful—until Zeke, a junior, went down on the football field. And did not get up.

As the paramedics rushed forward, Scott took the steps down to the field two at a time, bounded over the tall fence, and rushed to our son. I ran along behind him, my heart in my throat. Then I came face to face with the fence. *What to do, what to do?*

I stopped for a fleeting second and thought, *If I climb this fence and Zeke's okay, I'll embarrass my son for the rest of his mortal life. If I don't, I'll have to fight every mothering instinct in me that's telling me to go to my hurting child.*

What can I say? I'm a mom. I climbed.

When I got to the sidelines, Scott looked up and caught my eye, motioning for me to return to The Mother Spot—on the other side of the fence. He told me Zeke had dislocated his elbow, and I should run get the car and meet them at the hospital with insurance forms in hand.

I retraced my steps on legs of pure rubber; then, once again, I came to the fence. In the moments since I'd left it, it had GROWN. Try as I might, I could not get over the thing. So the cheerleaders gathered around me in pyramid formation and shoved me up and over the fence. I landed so hard that I injured my knee and couldn't get up. A kind man and good friend, Dane Woodall, had to help me off the field and drive me to the hospital. (Dane also discreetly pointed out that there was a gate not five yards from where I'd taken my undignified tumble.)

The feeling in my knee came back a while later, and though it was terribly sprained, I felt nothing until the next day—nothing hurt that night but my heart. Eventually, I hobbled over to the emergency room to see my son.

"Mom?" he asked as he lay, in terrible pain, arm outstretched and wrapped in splints, "why are you limping?"

I hopped on one leg until I was where I longed to be—with my arms around my child.

"I'm fine," I replied, "it's just a minor sports injury. No big deal."

Zeke looked confused, but I didn't explain. I just leaned on the clean white pillow, then stroked and kissed his cheek.

"I'm okay, Mom," he said courageously, "God was with me."

I forget that sometimes. But what a comforting thought. I can't be with my children, can't always protect them, though, Lord knows, I want to. Yet God's presence knows no bounds. He can be Father, Mother, Friend, and Brother to my kids—at least until I can hobble in to give them a kiss on the cheek.

●●◐◐◐

The following year, Zeke's senior year, our family had an amazing, awful experience of football déjá vu. Beautiful October Friday night, our red team playing blue team, Zeke goes down on the field. Paramedics arrive, Scott leaps the fence, but this time I wait and pray, out loud, behind the gate.

"It's his other elbow. Dislocated!" Scott shouts and we're off to the emergency room once more.

The next day, I e-mailed every mom I knew with the following SOS:

> I have some Good news and some Bad news. Good news: Lone Oak Buffaloes won 57-10 Friday night. They were 33-0 at the beginning of the second quarter when…Bad news:
>
> Zeke was injured again. Same heart-stopping scene: my son lying flat on his back on the field, paramedics coming out, I don't know if it's his head or arm or neck or back or what. (This time, however, I didn't climb the fence.) It was his other elbow—dislocated. We spent Friday in the emergency

room then had 25 football players over. (Zeke had planned a big party before the game—little Rachel and Gabe cooked burgers and hosted it!)

He's going to be okay—after a few weeks of healing. But his heart is just broken, and, because to have a child is to have your heart go walking around outside your body, ours is too. He LOVES this game, sacrificed everything to be on the team, was a star player—and now this, his senior year. We have some really painful decisions to make about continuing or not after this latest injury.

I can't take any more scenes of my son lying on the field like that. Scott, too, says "no more" to me, in private—but we're waiting for doctor's report, hoping he will get to be the bad guy instead of us. The harder part is watching Zeke hurting emotionally too—thinking of him watching from the sidelines aching to be with the team.

Please pray for him. Bless his little angelic heart, between tears (not from pain, but from disappointment), he said, "If it isn't God's will for me to play, I want to do something meaningful with my time. Maybe volunteer at the hospital or work with kids or do charity work." And I'm thinking, God, did this kid come with invisible wings? (He sure didn't come with very good joints…)

Love,
Heartbroken, but grateful, Mommie

Over the next few days, I got messages from sports moms and friends from all over the country. "We're praying for Zeke," "I know just how you feel, Becky, I remember when our son …" And wonderful messages from men friends, too, who poignantly recalled their own senior year and various sports-related triumphs over tragedies.

I felt somehow connected to every mother and father who understood.

The doctor eventually fitted Zeke with two robotic-like devices to protect his elbows, and he played the last two games of the season with typical resiliency, courage, and joy.

I didn't know whether to cry or cheer, and watched most of those last two games from behind my hands—only daring to peek now and again between my fingers.

Finding ourselves stuck in motherhood, we trudge forward toward cold, hard bleachers, lukewarm coffee in hand, to cheer our kids on and pray for their safety and heave a huge sigh of relief when the season is over.

In May of Zeke's senior year (completed, thank God, with no more injuries), Scott and I went to the school sports banquet. The head coach announced that they only give one award each year: to the team member who has overcome obstacle after obstacle. "The award," he said, visibly moved with emotion, "is called The Fighting Heart Award. And this year that special award goes to Zeke Freeman."

What can I say? I'm a mom. I cried.

Postscript: In May 1999, Zeke walked out the door, rock climbing gear slung over his shoulder, and waved a cheerful goodbye as he headed off to college in San Marcos, Texas. And a piece of my heart went out the door with him.

However, it comes back home one or two weekends a month, attached to two enormous bags of laundry.

Listen my son...

When you walk, your steps will not be hampered;

when you run, you will not stumble.

Hold on to instruction, do not let it go; guard it well, for it is your life.

PROVERBS 4:10-13

The mother-child relationship is paradoxical and, in a sense, tragic. It requires the most intense love on the mother's side, yet this very love must help the child grow away from the mother and to become fully independent.

—Eric Fromm

20

Father of the Little Girl Bride

The phone woke me from a sound sleep. I checked the clock through sleep-laden eyes. 7:00 A.M.

"Hello?" I said, awake but not fully aware.

"Becky, it's Melissa. Have you heard?"

"Have I heard what?"

"Our kids are officially boyfriend and girlfriend."

"Rachel and Joshua?"

"Yes!"

"But they've just been buddies, pals, boy-and-girl-next-door all these years."

"Well, wake up and smell the romance. Josh asked her to go with him and she said yes and do you know what that means???"

"What?"

"We could be mothers-in-law someday."

I sat up in bed and blinked to let the vision of our two children in front of a stained glass window focus more clearly in my mind. I could just barely make out Rachel with her golden curls silhouetted by a white lace veil, and Josh, tanned and handsome, standing waiting for his bride in a black tuxedo. "We could be, couldn't we? Mothers-in-law, I mean."

"Do you think this calls for coffee?"

"Of course! I'll put on the Folgers, we meet at my kitchen table in 20 minutes."

Within the hour, Melissa and I were sipping at our steaming mugs, munchin' on bagels, and discussing the futures of our children, grandchildren, and great-grandchildren. The news of our childrens' recent pairing transformed us from best friends and neighbors (we call ourselves "Lucy and Ethel") into two Yentas. It all felt so Yiddish, sitting across the table, future mothers of the bride and groom. I wished for a scarf and an apron and a thick foreign accent, for I was really in the mood for meddling.

"You know what's really great?" I asked, a comforting thought crossing my mind.

"No, what?" asked Melissa.

"You and I have known each other so long and have been through so much family trauma together that the kids know all about our mutual family shortcomings. There'll be no surprises after the honeymoon is over."

"That's right," answered Melissa, brightening at the thought. Then raising one eyebrow, and doing an expert imitation of Freud, she added, "And da dysfunctions ve know are much better dan de dysfunctions ve don't know."

By the time we'd planned the wedding, the honeymoon, named the grandbabies, and planned when and where Rach and Josh could spend their holidays, it occurred to us that Rachel was, after all, only 15. And Josh, though a fairly mature 16, didn't look anywhere near ready to tackle a mortgage on the Victorian house we'd mentally built and decorated (located, of course, equidistant from each mother-in-law).

As it turned out, the courtship of Josh and Rachel was a brief-but-sweet romance. After a summer of selling snow-cones and skiing around the lake together, the nip in the autumn air reminded our kids that, after all, they were 15 and 16. Though they cared for each other, neither was ready to call a halt to the pleasures of flirting once they started back to school. Rachel cried off and on for 24 hours, a ritual all 15-year-old girls are allowed to indulge in at the end of a first love. The breakup had been as gentle as possible, both pledging to remain friends. Then with me singing old movie tunes "Many a new day will dawn ..." and "I'm gonna wash that man right outta my hair"—in the background, Rachel dried her tears, washed her face, and applied fresh mascara and lipstick. She slipped on her favorite faded blue jeans and a soft pink sweater, filling them out as only girls in their prime can do. Then she gracefully sailed off to enjoy the other fish in the freshman sea.

For Melissa and me, it was the end of an era of ploytzing. Reluctantly, we put our imaginary golden-haired grandaughters and dark-eyed grandsons to bed in our heads. Though we stand ever ready should the occasion call for a pair of neighboring, meddling mothers-in-law, we realize, for now, we have to let our kids make their own decisions about dating and romance and marriage.

By the time Rachel actually grows up and gets married, I wonder how many weddings and grandbabies I'll have imagined into and out of existence.

Scott, on the other hand, wants to hear none of this non-sense. I think, in his mind, he believes Rachel will stay home and keep her daddy wrapped around her little finger indef-initely. And yet, he does know there will come a day when, with his daughter at his side, he'll hear a preacher ask, "Who gives this woman to be wed?" Though he'll be tempted, Scott knows he can't shuffle his feet, give a sideways glance, and mumble, "Nobody."

To bolster himself for the inevitable, Scott gave Rachel one half of a golden heart-shaped charm for her twelfth birthday. "When the right young man asks you to marry him someday," Scott told Rach, "give him your half of the heart as a symbol that he's the one you've chosen to spend your life with. When he comes to ask me for your hand, I'll ask to see the charm and then give him my half, so you two will have the whole heart of my blessing. Until that day, I'll hold on to it for safe keeping."

Last week, Scott and I had the privilege of hearing Steve and Annie Chapman perform in concert. Since Rachel was old enough to put a cassette in the stereo, she and her daddy have claimed Steve's *You're the Only Little Girl in My Heart* as "their song." To our delight, Steve sang this song during the concert. It's a song that talks about a father playing a little game with his small daughter. As she does a charming ballerina twirl, he asks her, "Who's the only man in your heart?" to which she answers, "Daddy, don't you know? You're the only man in my heart."

Then one day, as the father sees a schoolboy walking his daughter home, he feels a strange and jealous pain in his heart. When the boy finally walks away, the father asks if he might walk with his little girl for awhile. And they play their little game again. "Who's the only man in your heart?" And she says, "Daddy, don't you know, Daddy don't you know? You're the only man in my heart."

Then comes the inevitable: the wedding day. A young man slips a ring on the daughter's hand. And the father knows, deep inside, he's no longer the only man in his little girl's heart. But for old time's sake, they still play the little game again.

At this point in the song, as Steve strummed his guitar and sang the sweet refrain, I looked up at Scott and saw a tear trickle its way down his check. I saw this same look on his face as we watched a scene from the movie *Father of the Bride*. If you've seen the movie, and you're a father, you know the part. It's the poignant scene where father and daughter play one last, late-night game of basketball before another man walks the young lady down the aisle toward her new life. It's a bittersweet reality for fathers.

Why do mothers look forward to their daughter's wedding day, "ploytzing" about the details, while a father's first impulse is to grab a shotgun and point it in the direction of any young man coming to court his daughter?

Perhaps it's because we women know we don't really have to share our daughters. She'll continue to come to us for motherly advice, perhaps even more so as she slips into the new roles of wife, and eventually, mother. But for daddies…it seems that nothing will ever be quite the same. His daughter has a new hero, a new protector in her life. Where does a dad go after the wedding day?

Hopefully, nowhere. The nice surprise is that even after a woman grows up, marries, and has babies of her own, she still needs her father's love. Some things never change.

There's not a woman alive who doesn't long to know that she was, is, and always will be a precious little girl in the heart of her father. Whether that father holds a basketball or a heart-shaped charm—or a galaxy of stars in the palm of His hand.

Many daughters have done well, but you excel them all.

PROVERBS 31:29 NKJV

Certain it is that there is no kind of affection so purely angelic as that of a father to his daughter. He beholds her both with and without regard to her sex. In love to our wives there is desire; to our sons there is ambition; but in that to our daughters there is something which there are no words to express.
—Joseph Addison

Three Simple Rules for Dating My Daughter

Rule One: If you pull into my driveway and honk, you'd better be delivering a package, because you're sure not picking anything up.

Rule Two: In order for us to get to know each other, we *should* talk about sports, politics, and other issues of the day. Please do not do this. The only information I require from you is an indication of when you expect to have my daughter safely back at my house, and the only word I need from you on this subject is "early."

Rule Three: I have no doubt you are a popular fellow, with many opportunities to date other girls. This is fine with me as long as it is okay with my daughter. Otherwise, once you have gone out with my little girl, you will continue to date no one but her until she is finished with you. If you make her cry, I will make you cry.

21

Grace for Gurus

My oldest son, Zach, is home for a visit. He's 19 and has a nifty, off-putting collection of piercings on his eyebrow and chin, and what he currently believes to be the wisdom of the ages between his ears. I listen as he defines in exhaustive detail the problems of mankind, the evil in the world, his determination to overcome it all with peace, love, and goodness—plus his special-serving, deep, inner knowledge.

I nod softly and think, *My son, the prophet.*

"But people are afraid of me!" he says, raising his voice in defiance. "They judge me solely on the way I look!"

I refrain from saying, "If I randomly poked holes in my head and stuck curtain rings through them, I suppose I, too, would get a certain odd reaction from others." Instead I say, "That's why God made mothers."

"What?" he asks, momentarily distracted from his rantings on the downward spiraling of the world. I can't help but think of Goethe's famous statement, "Everyone believes in his youth that the world really began with him."

"It's impossible for someone who diapered your bottom to be afraid of you, no matter how old you get to be or how much hardware you loop through your skin."

At this, his scowl melts into a boyish grin. The little peanut-butter kid I once hugged and kissed goodnight is still inside this 19-year-old puzzle of a young man. The atmosphere around us relaxes at once, like a balloon released of its contents. "Mom, that's what I love about you."

"What's that?"

"You are so simpleminded and sweet that even I can't intimidate you."

I decide to take this as a compliment, kiss his one unpierced brow, and offer to fix him a sandwich. My guru-son follows me to the kitchen, temporarily dropping the weight of the world, and picks up a lighter load. Eyeing the peanut butters, he asks felicitously, "Why do they say choosy mothers choose Jif? I mean, what are they trying to imply?"

I roll my eyes with all the Shakespearean flair I can muster and, with a peanut-butter-dipped-dagger, respond, "To jelly, or not to jelly, THAT is the question."

The guru smiles a weary, grateful smile and simply says, "To jelly."

He doesn't realize quite yet that it isn't prophets or poets or philosophers or pilgrims who hold the secrets to the universe. It's God, working through courageous mothers—armed with plenty of peanut butter and prayer.

For nervous mothers of teens, a note of encouragement: Within three months, the earrings came out, replaced by an Abe Lincoln beard and a cowboy hat. Now if only the tattoo on his foot could come off as easily…

Be joyful in hope, patient in affliction, faithful in prayer.

ROMANS 12:12

Don't laugh at a youth for his affections; he's only trying on one face after another till he finds his own.
—**Logan Pearsall Smith**

Teen Angel

Isabel, surrounded by her laughing, talking, camera-toting sisters, helps her tiny daughter, Candy, into a diminutive pink formal. *My baby is so beautiful,* she thinks, wanting to laugh and cry and praise God all in one breath. Her handsome husband, Diego, gently takes one of Candy's small hands in his. Isabel reaches for her other hand. The couple smile at each other, the look in their eyes affirming, "Yes, life is good." Together they walk their little girl out the back door and down the porch steps.

Suddenly there's music, soft and up tempo, pouring from a nearby stereo...

"The moment I wake up..."

Candy's big eyes absorb the scene around her as she giggles and claps her joy.

"Before I put on my makeup..."

Smiling children, grasping pink and white balloons, line the long carpet in front of her. Most of them are Candy's cousins, born from the enormous living, laughing, loving embrace that is the "Familia Garcia Hernandez." One of them is her big brother, 17-year-old Ezequiel, and though he's only a year older than his sister, he towers above her, protective—his gorgeous smile, so like his mother's, an added blessing to the festivities.

"I say a little prayer for you…"

The song was Isabel's choice, one she sang to Candy in happy, homey moments.

It seemed such a long time since the day Isabel gave birth to this living blessing. Though, at the time, Isabel recalled, she hadn't thought of her baby in such holy terms. She remembered how she'd asked the nurses to let her hold and breastfeed her new baby soon after the birth, and how they had avoided Isabel's question, wanting to shield the new mother from going into shock at the sight of her newborn.

Finally, the nurses explained—24 hours later—that her daughter couldn't nurse, that she had a small problem with her mouth. "Just a tiny little cut," one of her sisters had reassured her. "Nothing that can't be fixed," another sister chimed in. When the nurses brought the feather-light, four-pound bundle wrapped in soft flannel for Isabel to see, she'd immediately looked up and said, "Bring me my baby with the tiny little cut. This one has no lip! Bring me a baby that looks like Ezequiel looked."

The cleft palate turned out to be the least of Candy's long list of medical complications that would leave her mind profoundly retarded and her body half the size of her peers'. How dark that day had seemed, but now, with the passage of time, it was clear how much love this child had tugged out of Isabel's heart! Out of all their hearts.

The music stopped as the family took their seats. The affair almost seemed like an outdoor wedding—in childlike miniature. The pastor, Isabel's brother-in-law, stood to read a note Isabel had prepared for this, her daughter's sixteenth birthday.

"We would like to thank every one of you who were able to make it to this very special occasion. To our friends and families that have, along with our family, witnessed a miracle in the making. It seems we have lived a lifetime of persistency, but with great rewards at the end of each goal. I will never forget the first miracle with Candy, the one that remains forever vivid in my mind.

"I wanted my little girl to show me some affection. I knew that everyone needed to be loved, so that meant my baby girl needed love, too. Time and time again...all I wanted was for her to return a kiss, pleading with her every time to please show me that my love for her was truly felt. Every morning of Candy's life, she has been awakened with a kiss. During the day I could not touch her enough.

"I was in her room on her bed one morning. Like always, I began stroking her head and her little arms, bending down to kiss her. My kisses were soft, soft enough that just in case she could return my kiss someday, I would feel it. This miracle morning, I felt it. Yes! She did...she kissed me! Ever so softly, but it was...it was...a kiss.

"And so began our journey of love. Goals to set, and thank GOD, goals that were met. Thank You, Jesus, for my little angel."

●●○●○

My own daughter, Rachel, has fallen into the welcoming embrace of the Garcia family. Dashing Ezequiel has been Rachel's boyfriend, off and on, for almost a year. Whether they're dating or not, their friendship remains strong and good. We couldn't ask for a better dating situation, for the Garcias generally move in clusters. Mom, Dad, sister,

"Grandma Ma-ma," and cousins often all come along with Ezequiel to pick up Rachel for their group date to the movies or a family fiesta. Their family, all devoted to God, started a bilingual church. Today they fill the pews to overflowing with mostly their own relatives—plus a couple of gringos, like my fair-skinned daughter.

Rachel adores the whole enchilada: the little church that meets in a one-room building; the simple, crowded fun of six people on a couch watching old movies; or 20 people bumping into each other in a cozy kitchen, trying to get to the tamales or the simmering pot of menudo. (Menudo is one thing Rachel refuses to touch. All she knows is that there's something floating in the fragrant stew that looks slimy and deeply suspicious.)

But mostly she loves the LOVE. "Momma," Rachel explained one day, "the way the whole family is with Candy is just so sweet. We'll be driving along, and Isabel will say to her 'Do you know you are my precious little girl? I love you so much.' Diego and Ezequiel are so kind to her, too. It's like a little angel has come into their home and filled it up with extra cups of love."

And so, she did.

Angels come in many forms. Some arrive in lightning white with wondrous wings.

And some arrive, without an upper lip, in tiny four-pound frames.

Some limp into the world on misshapen legs.

And some come with almond-shaped eyes, flat little noses, and chubby arms outstretched, perpetually posed for a hug.

But all come with one message to share: You were created to be loved and to love. Not because you're pretty or smart or fast or strong. But simply because you belong to God's family.

For you formed my inward parts; You covered me in my mother's womb. I will praise You, for I am fearfully and wonderfully made; marvelous are Your works, and that my soul knows very well. How precious also are Your thoughts to me, O God!

PSALM 139:13,14,17 NKJV

Jay, my son with Down syndrome, has proved to be a superior contender in life, and he has taught me so much about love. Today when I ask why, I ask with a totally different perspective. I ask, "Why, God? Why am I so blessed with this beautiful, sensitive child? How could You entrust me with this tender creation?"

From the Gold Medallion award-winning
EXTRAORDINARY KIDS: NURTURING AND CHAMPIONING
YOUR CHILD WITH SPECIAL NEEDS
**by Cheri Fuller and Louise Tucker Jones
(Focus/Tyndale, 1997).**

I highly recommend this joyful book for all mothers of special-needs kids. Another precious book is Angel Behind the Rocking Chair *by Pam Vredevelt.*

Just Because You're You

They say some babies born will only be
a heavy burden to a family
Because they'll never act the proper way,
so find a place for them to stay...

But a mother looks through tear filled eyes
and begins to sing this lullaby...

"I don't love you, for what you can, or cannot do
I love you, just because you're you
though many others may question your worth,
I'll treasure you, more than all the earth."

And when we see our soul so scared with sin
We are surprised to find God takes us in
For all we have to give Him is our shame
and though we fail the Lord, we hear Him say,

"Though I look at you through tear filled eyes,
I still sing to you this lullaby,

" 'I don't love you, for what you can or cannot do
I love you, just because you're you,
Though sometimes, you may question your own worth,
I'll love you, more than all the earth.' "

Original lyrics by my friend, Faye Yates written for her beautiful daughter who has Down syndrome. Faye's music tapes, her singing schedule, and Faye's touching book about mothering a Down child can be ordered at: Faye Yates Ministries, P.O. Box 34092, San Antonio, Texas 78265.

One More Story, Please
Grape Juice Communion

"Let the children come unto Me...for such is the kingdom of God."

The yellow schoolbus pulled up in front of our lakeside home and yawned two dozen kids into the yard. Our backporch —with its scenic view—had been chosen as a backdrop for school pictures this year. I walked outside to greet the kids, thankful the photos would be taken out-of-doors, since the "scenic view" inside my house had that Hurried American Ransacked look.

Just then, I noticed James—a small, grinning, mentally handicapped student— walking as he held his teacher's hand. James was not a member of this particular class, but his Special Ed. teacher thought he'd enjoy tagging along on this country field trip.

While the other kids shuffled off to the back yard, I invited James and his teacher inside for a snack. I offered the only thing I had on hand—a pitiful slice of my home-made bread. The bread had not risen and was the texture of Playdough left out in the sun. The teacher wisely declined, but James reached for a slice, took a bite, lifted his face toward heaven and pronounced it "WON-durful, WON-durful!" Curious, I took a bite. Sure enough, it tasted like Playdough left out in the sun.

But to James, my cooking disaster was manna from heaven.

"Would you like some grape juice?" I asked. James nodded, held out his hands, and took the glass of shimmering purple. Then, reverently bowing his head, he said, "Let us pray." I did as I was told. "Dear Lord, Dear Lord, Dear Lord," James intoned his fervent blessing. "For Your precious blood we are so thankful. You are good to us. In Jesus' Name, Amen."

When the prayer ended, I looked at James' teacher, smiled, and asked, "Is he always like this?"

"Oh, yes," she nodded. "James is my sunshine. I'm supposed to be his teacher, but the truth is I'm the one who's blessed."

Together, we marveled at this child who saw sacrament in flat bread and turned ordinary juice into holy communion.

Becky Freeman

Take-Out Laughs

W e've all watched movies and felt sad when they ended, and then—sometimes—the producers surprise us with a bonus treat. We get a peek at the "outtakes." Well, I think it's time we do that in book publishing as well. My wonderful, wacky, creative sister, Rachel, came aboard as assistant editor on this project helping me meet an unbelievably short deadline—and making the whole process seem more like play than work. Mostly because she makes me laugh, even as we work. And she's a wonderful encourager, peppering her e-mails with comments like, "This was really good. I didn't change it much. Will you pay me to just give you compliments?"

She never dreamed any of her little comments would see an audience of more than one (me) so be assured, none of the following was planned or contrived. This is my sister just as she is.

I sent the following chapter to her via e-mail (I've condensed it a bit) without running it through the spell check. As you'll see, spelling and accurate typing is not my forte. And now, a word from my smart aleck editing sister. (Her words are in bold, inside the < >s)

Outtakes from "Irrational Conception"

"I consdier**<consider>** warnign**<warning her that she won't ever be able to spell simple words again—just teasin' Beck>** her that she will never again read a newspaper without asking, 'What if that had been MY child?'

"I look at her carefully manicured nails and stylish suit and think that no matter how sophisticated she is, becoming a mother will reduce her to the primitive level of a bear protecting her cub...

"I feel I should warn her that no matter how many years she has invested ine **<in—or be consistent and use Nell language, "ine her careerie">**her career, she will be professionally derealed **<derailed>**by motherhood....one day she will be going into an important business meeting and she wil **<will>**think of her baby's sweet smell...

"Looking at my attractive friend, I want to asure **<assure her that I really mean that she may never spell correctly again>**her that eventually she will shed the pounds of pregnancy, but she will never feel the same about herself; that her life, now so important, will be of less value to her once she has a child...

"...that she...will bgin**<begin> <o.k. I'm laughing out loud now—are you alrite, I mean alright?>**to hope for more years—not to accomplish her own dreams, but to wtch**<watch> <I'm wheezing now—alone at 1 a.m., doubled over in laughter!>**her child accomplish theirs...

"I want to describe to my friend the exhilaraion**<exhilaration> <I'm crying now>**of seeing your child learn to ride a bike. I want to capture for ther **<her>**the belly laugh of a baby who is touching the soft fur of a dog or cat for the first time. I want her to tast**<taste> <or "chickabee tast the hunybee">**the joy that is so real, it actually hearts**<hurts>**

<or it will work as hearts if you imply a nervy New Yorker accent>

"My friend's quizzical look makes me realize that tears have formed in my eyes.

"You'll never regret it", **<inside quotes?>**I finally say...

And that is exactly, though perhaps not as eloquently**<whew, I'll say!>**, what I finally **<thank God>**....

We passed a miniature polka dotted swimsuit,**<B, forgive me, but I was thinking "passed" like one passing a gall stone>**.

Vanilla, Strawberry, or Chocolate Chili Pepper?

Becky Freeman is famous for observing (and experiencing) the crazy and compassionate, the delight and doubt, and the love and laughter of life. *Chocolate Chili Pepper Love* is a heartwarming collection of fun ideas and hilarious tales that will bring smiles of joy and a new perspective to your marriage.

Discover:

- the differences between an easy "vanilla" marriage, a fun "strawberry" marriage, and the excitement of a "chocolate–chili pepper" marriage

- the keys to making a high-maintenance relationship successful

- how to have fun even in the difficult times

Finding a good dose of humor and hope amid the clutter of kids and romantic moments gone wrong, Becky reminds you that marriage is a journey to be celebrated.